Does Canada Need A New Electoral System?

Queen's Studies on the
Future of the
Canadian Communities

1

Does Canada Need A New Electoral System?

William P. Irvine

Institute of
Intergovernmental
Relations

Queen's University
Kingston, Ontario
Canada

© 1979, William P. Irvine

ISSN 0708-3289
ISBN 0-88911-011-5

Queen's Studies on the Future of the Canadian Communities is a monograph series based on research funded by the Donner Canadian Foundation.

Distributed by P.D. Meany Company Incorporated,
Box 534, Port Credit, Ontario L5G 4M2

Typesetting: Eastern Typesetting Company, Kingston, Ontario

Printed in Canada by: Brown & Martin, Limited, Kingston, Ontario

To my parents, who have kept Scots and French together for a long time.

Contents

Foreword

This study is the first in a series of monographs to be published under the general title: Queen's Studies on the Future of the Canadian Communities. W.P. Irvine has developed a persuasive case for substantial modification of the Canadian electoral system in the direction of greater proportionality. He clearly demonstrates some of the perverse effects of the present system. It accentuates the regional imbalances in party support, and underrepresents important segments of opinion in the House of Commons and cabinet.

This analysis leads him to propose a revised system. He carefully explores the range of alternatives available to policy-makers, and examines in detail their pros, cons and likely effects in the Canadian context. In choosing a "topping up" method, in which a pool of party list candidates would be available to bring into line proportions of seats and votes, Irvine is sensitive to the broad range of values — from representation to stable government — served by electoral systems. He also demonstrates his awareness that the effect of institutional rules is heavily dependent on the character of the society in which they are implanted. Finally, he explores the political forces which may be mobilized for and against major change in our method of selecting our representatives. His monograph is thus not only a significant contribution to the debate on constitutional change in the Canadian federation, but also is an important addition to the study of elections and electoral systems generally. It will be of interest to many students of comparative politics, democratic theory and political sociology.

As a constitutional option, electoral system change is rooted in the conception that one important source of regional alienation and discontent lies in the loss of the ability of the central government adequately to represent and take account of the interests of citizens of all regions. This is most sharply demonstrated by the increasing regionalization of party support. That, in turn, is both fostered and exacerbated by the way the first-past-the-post electoral system exaggerates the regional imbalance in party support at the Parliamentary level. The result is a greater sense of alienation among citizens of those regions who are underrepresented, and who find they have few representatives in the governing party caucus and cabinet. This underrepresentation may also have deleterious effects on party policy formulation and party electoral strategies — making them less sensitive to regions and groups who carry little weight in party caucuses.

Proposals, like Irvine's, for electoral reform, are thus aimed both at ensuring broad representation within all parties, and at altering the structure of incentives that face party strategists. Such proposals — and Irvine's is the most carefully spelled out yet to appear — are hence aimed at politically strengthening the centre. It joins some other proposals, such as an elected Senate and modification of party discipline in the House of Commons, which are also designed to revitalize the central government. All these proposals suggest that the preferred direction for constitutional change is to revitalize the integrative capacity of Ottawa, rather than to embrace large-scale decentralization.

Canadians, especially those who hold, or have held office, may well be reluctant to tamper with a set of institutions bequeathed to us from Britain, and which have served us well. Yet any serious attempt to think through how we can maintain or strengthen its legitimacy in the future must consider changes such as those suggested here. And they must also consider other ways in which political parties may better serve as integrative forces, bridging regional and sectional interests, and linking together politics at the federal and provincial levels. Institutional tinkering alone is not enough. Irvine's careful proposals address these problems, but are also highly sensitive to the values other than national integration which must guide party activity. They deserve careful consideration from all concerned citizens.

The Irvine study represents one important strategy for change. Others will be explored in subsequent monographs in the Queen's Studies on the Future of the Canadian Communities. These studies are the first of a series of research projects carried out by scholars at Queen's University, coordinated by the Institute of Intergovernmental Relations. They grew out of the first look at many of these problems, published shortly after the election of the *Parti Québécois* as *Must Canada Fail?*

The studies, while by no means exploring all major dimensions of the challenge of working out the political future of French and English-speakers, Quebec and the rest of Canada, and the various regional communities, seek to illuminate many of them. Subsequent monographs will explore the character of the alternatives and proposals that have been put forward; consider the lessons to be drawn from other federations and plural societies; assess the consequences of both existing federal arrangements and possible alternative structures for a wide variety of contemporary policy problems; examine the multiple bases of political community in Canada; explore the limits and possibilities of "association" between sovereign states; examine the procedures we now use for major constitutional changes, and possible changes in them; speculate on the ways of imagining constitutional futures and the twenty-first century; and critically assess the complex and difficult question of the costs and benefits of economic integration.

All the monographs will try to bridge the world of the academic and that of the citizen policy-maker — seeking both to advance knowledge of the basic political processes at work and to communicate these insights to those who must make the decisions.

These projects, and publication of the monographs, have been made possible by a generous grant from the Donner Canadian Foundation, for which we are very grateful. All studies are solely the responsibility of their individual authors.

Richard Simeon.
Director,

Institute of
Intergovernmental Relations,
Queen's University.

Preface

Canada's central institutions face a crisis of representation. This has led to a marked loss of legitimacy and hence authority of the federal cabinet, the federal parliament and the federal judiciary. They are less able to carry through the kinds of accommodation necessary if the country is to survive.

The election results of May 22, 1979 underline the crisis dramatically. They demonstrate the critical need to search for mechanisms by which to assure all major regional and linguistic groups of representation in the caucus and cabinet of the governing party in Ottawa.

This study proposes a major change in Canada's electoral system. Such a reform would go a long way towards guaranteeing both Westerners and Quebeckers a place in the governing party. No longer would elections be about which segment might be excluded from the federal government. This should increase the legitimacy and authority of the federal government in both areas.

This monograph was completed before the federal election was called. The results of that election – briefly analyzed in Appendix C – strengthen the conclusions I reached. The polarization of the vote and the weakening of a major party in some region is even more pronounced than ever before. In much of the west, the Liberal vote has slipped to the point where the present electoral system denies them any parliamentary representation at all. But for the force of two local candidates, the same is true for the Progressive Conservatives in Quebec.

Not since 1917 has a governing party had so few members in Quebec. The West is now solidly represented in government – but it has been frozen out in the past and will be again unless structural reforms to the party system are made. Changing the electoral system changes the incentives under which political parties operate. With the proper incentives, parties can build organizations in all parts of the country and become more sensitive to the feelings and interests of all Canadians.

Under the present system, the ability of both the Liberal and the Progressive Conservative parties to rebuild in their weak regions was seriously weakened by the election results. Both parties lost many young and able candidates — people who could have added fresh faces and new support to the parties that nominated them.

What are the chances of electoral system reform? On page 72 are listed four conditions which would make it more probable. Only one is clearly ruled out by the 1979 results: Liberal support in Quebec has not yet been seriously threatened despite PQ support for the *Créditistes* and the presence of the nationalist *Union Populaire*. Canada has a minority government in which swing parties could call for electoral system reform. Such reform will be resisted by the major parties but may seem increasingly attractive if the minority situation persists over several elections. The NDP does hold a balance of power position, but is not the only party to do so. It has called for such reform in the past, and could try to bargain for it. The fourth condition, English/French polarization in both the House of Commons and the electorate, is painfully visible.

The politics of electoral system reform is complicated, and the prospects of reform did receive a setback on May 22nd. The governing party now has fewer popular votes than the major opposition party. This does not usually happen under our present electoral system. It is traceable to the regionalism of the country, as is demonstrated in Appendix C. Whatever its sources, it does mean that the Progressive Conservative government might be more reluctant to embark on an electoral reform that would have denied it victory in 1979. However, the sweetness of that victory is diminished by their drop in popular vote in Quebec. Outside Quebec, the Progressive Conservatives are the largest single party and have been since 1972. They should see electoral system reform as a way of increasing not only their representation in Quebec but their overall popular vote as well.

Any move to a more proportional electoral system would make minority or coalition government more probable than it has been so far. Though usually offered as the main argument against reform, the predictability of minority government should be seen as an asset. Under the present electoral system, minority governments weigh electoral calculations heavily. Large parties try to build up a record that might produce a majority outcome next time. Minor parties fear the loss of their identity and of their best policies if they allow the minority government a long hold on office. They risk the opprobrium of having precipitated an election if they defeat the government too quickly. Good government may emerge from all this calculation and manoeuvering. It has in the past — but only as a bye-product, and often at the price of subordinating the long-run interest of the country to the short-run electoral interest of the party.

This work would not have been written at all had not Richard Simeon, the Director of the Institute of Intergovernmental Relations, interrupted my sabbatical in Italy with a letter saying that there was some interest in electoral system reform as a possible element in restructuring Canadian political institutions and suggesting that I think about it. The following pages record those thoughts, much enriched by the careful reading that Richard Simeon and Edwin Black gave to an earlier version of the text. I also benefitted from comments on a much shorter paper presented to a Workshop on the Political Economy of Confederation, jointly sponsored by the Institute of Intergovernmental Relations and the Economic Council of Canada.

The first draft of this monograph was written at the European University Institute. My thinking on electoral systems, party systems and the contribution of both to government was much influenced by the intellectual life there, particularly by Professor Hans Daalder's seminar on political parties and his workshop on post-war changes in European party systems. I am grateful for Professor Daalder's and the Institute's hospitality during my sabbatical and to the Social Sciences and Humanities Research Council for a sabbatical leave fellowship.

I should also like to record my thanks to Mrs. Bernice Gallagher for the very prompt and careful work she did on various versions of this monograph. Mrs. Carol Ann Pentland was a most skilled editor. The text is much improved as a result of her careful work.

With such talented assistance and advice, there should be few remaining faults. Any partiality of treatment or questionable judgements are my own.

William P. Irvine,
Queen's University.

William P. Irvine is Associate Professor of Political Studies at Queen's University. He is author of numerous articles on elections and party systems.

1 Introduction

Many features of the Canadian political and constitutional system rest to a large extent on inheritance and tradition. One of the salutary effects of the November 1976 election in Quebec has been to force Canadians to take a second look at these institutions to see if any better justification is possible or to see if modifications might be desirable. In an imperfect world with people neither impartial nor ignorant of their own interests, political institutions raise as many questions of engineering as they do of morals. There is no uniquely and universally desirable constitutional division of power, method of court appointment, or electoral system. Rather, we must decide what we want to accomplish and marshall the best available knowledge as to how to bring about those ends. This is, in general, the approach to be followed in this monograph. In arguing that Canada should adopt a new method of counting votes, it will review data on both the strength of the present Canadian party system and on the functioning of different types of electoral systems elsewhere.

In the past few years, all Canadians have felt a sharpening of the tension among three forces which Richard Simeon has characterized as "country-building, province-building, and Quebec nation-building" (Evenson and Simeon 1978; Simeon, 1978). As the labels imply, these are thrusts, at both the mass and elite levels, aimed at extending the range of decision-making authority of federal or provincial governments. Each force has an affective component as well, but the last two forces are distinguished by the intensity of that component. Though all provinces have special interests and grievances about their capacity to deal with these areas of interest, Quebec can add to this an especially strong sense of self-identity and self-assertion as an entity distinct from its neighbours.

Country-building, province-building and Quebec nation-building

1

are tendencies which have coexisted throughout Canadian history, but have varied in relative force. Most recently, country-building was the dominant force after the Second World War. It began somewhat hesitantly during the Depression but found its major impetus in the mobilization of wealth, manpower and resources for combat. Although most of the war-time apparatus was dismantled after 1945, the initial momentum persisted for some fifteen years. A fear of post-war economic dislocation, coupled with a highly talented Ottawa civil service committed to Keynesian economic management and proud of its wartime accomplishments, sustained this trust. At the popular level, total war always seems to generate support for new social organization and Canada after 1945 was no exception. That and the world-wide economic boom provided mass support for country-building, support that, to some extent, cut across cultural and regional divisions.

We now know that this was not an inexorable self-sustaining process. Province-building and Quebec nation-building tendencies were submerged but not eliminated during the 1950's. They came to dominate the 1960's and 1970's under leaders whose education and major formative experiences occurred in the country-building decade. It is clear that these forces are not yet spent and that the 1980's will probably afford them greater institutional recognition. Legal authority over matters such as communications, immigration and economic development will devolve to provinces on either an exclusive or a shared basis. Provinces may obtain a greater role in the formation of central government policy as well.

What will happen to the centre in Canadian politics is not now predictable. Theoretically, one could do away entirely with an independent central power. Canada could become a confederation in the strict sense with matters settled through multilateral negotiation. It is not necessarily the case that such a change would produce major redirections of Canadian policy. What is clear is that such a development would seriously violate many of the beliefs, assumptions and interests of the Canadian people — the same set of beliefs, assumptions and interests which have influenced and been influenced by the country-building process in the past. Among these are self-definitions as heirs of a country stretching from sea to sea, a liberalism implying equal standing before government, whether one stands as a consumer of services or as a voter, and an egalitarianism designed to make the liberalism more effective (Irvine, 1977). Many of these beliefs and assumptions are spillovers of American political culture. As such, they affect English-speakers more than French-speakers, but the latter are certainly not immune to the moral claims implied in liberalism and egalitarianism. Policies now justified

2

on these moral grounds could possibly be shown to be consistent with self-interest. The liberalism supports a belief that Canadians must have a choice of cultural offerings insofar as these are publicly provided. Specifically, most English-speaking Canadians hold that people ought to be able to choose the language of education for their children and the language, content and source of media offerings. Though Quebec has now violated what would be defined as a liberal educational policy, the leaders of the *Parti Québécois* themselves see this as a transitional measure. It is entirely possible that a separate Quebec would discover that its self-interest required it to maximize the facility of its population in the use of English — even to the point of broadening access to schools in which English was the language of instruction. Similarly, in the richer provinces in Canada, being taxed to provide equalization payments is now justified in terms of a basic egalitarianism. It is quite probable that it could be justified in terms of self-interest. The enhanced standard of living made possible in poorer provinces by equalization payments makes them better consumers of products from the richer provinces.

While such possibilities exist, one doubts that self-interest can justify as many things to as many people as can now be based on a diffuse moral sense of community. However this may be, it is clear that the violation of these sensibilities would produce an intolerable short-run situation. In this short run, the response is likely to be punitive rather than self-interested. There will, as a result, be no basis for mutually beneficial policies or communitarian policies, and every likelihood of mutually destructive tendencies. This alone would provide sufficient justification to examine proposals aimed at restoring the legitimacy of the country-building force. If further justification were needed, it could be found in the position of Lord Acton, much quoted by Prime Minister Trudeau, to the effect that the coexistence of several thrusts within a single state generates a dynamic that is conducive both to liberty and to innovation and adaptability (Acton, 1956). Despite the fact that Acton was writing in the era of the "policeman state" and that he seemed to think that his multi-national state would, by virtue of its composition, not go beyond this limited role, the assumption of this monograph is that it is possible to re-establish the authority of a central government having a strong positive role in policy-making. The role will not necessarily be the same as the one it now has, but would still be considerable given pressures towards economic integration.

The system for casting and counting votes is not itself a prime determinant of the legitimacy or illegitimacy of a government except in the most blatant cases of effective disenfranchisement. In Canada, we would expect its effect to be transmitted through changes in the party system.

3

By reforming electoral rules, we can provide parties with both the incentives and the resources to follow certain courses of action, courses which would have beneficial consequences for increasing central authority.

Although any government is an inter-related whole, it is useful to analytically separate the input and output sides of the system. The growth of central authority will require development on both sides: growth in the legitimacy attached to the parties and parliamentarians linking citizens and governments, and growth in the responsiveness of the government.

Legitimacy requires a broadening of the representation of social groups in decision-making roles and a deepening of the institutional roots of government in the society. These may be partly conflicting goals: the party that appeals to all groups may not develop strong attachment to any one of them. Whether or not these goals are mutually inconsistent is a function of the extensiveness of the divisions of the country and of the width of these divisions. Legitimacy will be enhanced if we can devise a system capable of managing social conflict. This capacity and its cost are not only a function of institutional arrangements, however, but of the degree of social conflict in Canada. There is another source of legitimacy as well: tradition, familiarity, and procedural quality. In a country as culturally divided as Canada, these should not be sought as uppermost goals. Any new system will have its bugs, however, and it may be possible to offset the discontent generated by initial problems if it can be shown that the system preserves much of what we have been used to, that the link between our actions and electoral results is clear, and that outcomes do not turn on irrelevant considerations.

On the output side, governmental responsiveness is a function of two things. Governments must be able to make and to change policy: that is, they must be able to govern. Government must also afford groups and individuals opportunity for redress of consequences of government action where these are not derivative from policy. We may take for granted that any government will, in certain cases, act slowly, incompetently or arbitrarily. A government with the capacity and incentive to discover and correct these individual injustices will have more authority than one that does not.

Electoral systems have been extensively analyzed, and even more extensively argued about. Like the Canadian Confederation debates, the vast expenditure of intellectual energy and ability has not so far devised a system that is optimal from all points of view. In the third section of this monograph, we will compare electoral systems in terms of their effect on different components of governmental authority. In some cases we can evaluate effects in terms of the empirical evidence; in many others, evidence has not been gathered and the link will be provided only by a formal argument.

Before turning to the evidence, or logic, of the links between particular electoral systems and particular aspects of governmental authority, the next section will offer a brief review of electoral systems and a fuller exposition of the values that may be affected by the choice of one system rather than another. The fourth section will propose a new electoral system for Canada — a variant of the hybrid found in the Federal Republic of Germany — and compare it with certain other proposals in Canadian public debate. That the system here proposed offers the optimal (not the best) mix of consequences compared to other proposals or to other classic types of electoral system will be the argument of the fifth section. The monograph concludes with a discussion of the political feasibility of engineering electoral system reform in Canada.

After the present paragraph, little more will be said about rules for enfranchising voters or for drawing constituency boundaries. These subjects do affect who gets represented in Parliament and have been hotly debated in the past. If both the heat and the debate have died, it is due to the fact that we live in a system of effective cabinet government and only formal parliamentary government. Given that contending political interests in Canada are geographically concentrated, in the case of French speakers, or even geographically defined, as in the case of the Prairies, parliamentary representation necessarily reflects these units. So it does, with a quite strict eye to equality of numbers, hedged only by certain constitutional guarantees to Prince Edward Island and by concessions to the difficulty of travel in the sparsely populated areas of northern Canada. But parliament neither initiates nor otherwise determines public policy: that is done by cabinets and governing parties.

These *do not* represent all major interests in the country. They are also the central objects in the current crisis of central government authority. If their legitimacy and responsiveness can be enhanced, that of the central government will follow. Cabinets and parties live in a number of environments, one of which is the electoral arena. Others include the legal system, the communications networks around Ottawa, and their own electoral pasts. Not all of these offer equally fruitful points for intervention. This monograph explores the likely consequences of intervening to reshape the incentives set by the electoral system.

5

2 Electoral Systems and Values: An Overview

Specialists in electoral systems are no different from any other specialists: convinced of the importance of their subject matter, they easily find it manifesting itself in all important spheres of political life. As we shall see in the next section, not not all of these linkages are well established either logically or empirically. By way of introduction, however, it is worth reviewing some of these propositions, which can be grouped under six broad headings. Electoral systems are held to powerfully affect the way parties:

1. represent and mobilize opinion;
2. respond to the electorate;
3. select campaign tactics;
4. develop as organizations;
5. organize government to take appropriate action, to enact laws, etc.

In addition, an electoral system change has implications for traditions bearing on voting and governing.

Representation is hardly a passive process. Parties must decide how to define issues, and what positions to take up on those issues as defined. Alan Cairns has argued that the present electoral system gives parties an incentive to try to define issues in regional terms rather than in terms of social classes. As he put it:

> The frequently noted conservative tone which pervades Canadian politics is a consequence of the sectional nature of the party system. The emphasis on sectional divisions engendered by the electoral system has submerged class conflicts, and to the extent that our politics has been ameliorative it has been more

6

concerned with the distribution of burdens and benefits between sections than between classes. The poverty of the
Maritimes has occupied an honourable place in the foreground
of public discussion. The diffuse poverty of the generally un-
derprivileged has scarcely been noticed (Cairns, 1968, p. 74).

Having defined issues in Canada in regional-linguistic terms, do the
parties take up extreme positions on this spectrum or moderate ones?
Whatever they do, which strategy would the present electoral system
reward? Cairns opts for the position that the electoral system encourages
parties to stress regional distinctiveness and so to exacerbate our cleavages. The alternatives to the present electoral system all tend to reflect
votes more closely in assigning seats to parties, including new parties.
These alternative systems have many opponents who would disagree
with Cairns' analysis, or at least disagree that the situation could be
improved by a new electoral system. They tend to see the alternative
systems as subject to a kind of Say's Law, whereby extreme parties drive
out moderate ones (Hermens, 1941, pp. 15-30; Duverger, 1951, pp.
388-390).

There is another aspect to the representation question. Although issues may be defined and positions taken by parties, it is people who get
seats in parliament and cabinet. To what extent does an electoral system
increase the likelihood that certain groups of people will be elected? In
particular, could one (assuming one wanted to) design an electoral system more likely to elect Canadians who were members of relatively small
minorities: those who are neither English nor French for example?
Would the same system also reward minorities that might be considered
less deserving, at least by readers of this monograph: racists, or extremists of right or left?

Responsiveness to the electorate has many dimensions. Does the electoral system provide a clear and recognizable link between what the
voter has done (in marking his ballot) and the outcome of the election?
The system used in Canada is sensitive to the preferences of the electorate, but also to what may seem, to the voter, irrelevant considerations:
the number of candidates running, or the division among opponents
(Spafford, 1970; Johnston and Ballantyne, 1977). Beyond this, one might
ask if any electoral system encourages members of parliament to service
their constituents and be attentive to their problems between elections.
Finally, does any electoral system increase the capacity for change in a
political system where it is obvious that change would be needed to meet
the aspiration of the voters? Clearly, alienation from the federal government is not tied only to the national unity issue. Immobilist government
or arrogant government also increases the distance between citizens and

their rulers. Electoral systems have to be evaluated according to the impact they have on that distance.

What issues to emphasize and what political positions to take are strategic questions. They can only analytically be separated from a number of tactical questions bearing on campaigning. Given that a party has limited money, and that a party leader has only so much time and stamina, how should these resources be deployed during a campaign? Is this too, a question whose answer depends on the nature of the electoral system? Cairns argues that it is (Cairns, 1968, pp. 64-68). The Progressive Conservative party has seen its vote fluctuate around the 20% level in Quebec. The Liberal party has a comparable position on the Prairies. In both cases, few more seats could be won without a dramatic increase in the vote. If prospects for such breakthroughs are slim, tactics as well as strategy will be deployed to reinforce strength. A more proportional electoral system might reward a three to five percentage point increase in vote in an area of weakness. Moreover, campaigns are not just about the use of political resources. In the heat of a contest, under the present electoral system, candidates, if not leaders, find it irresistible to depart from the campaign high road. The Cairns analysis is full of examples. Elections since he wrote have not failed to generate new ones. While no one could doubt Robert Stanfield's commitment to biculturalism and the French fact in Canada, many of his candidates in 1972 found that references to French power and a contemptuous recitation of a litany of French-Canadian names were rhetorical devices which were real crowd-pleasers. When Liberal ministers were criticized for ineptness, or party contributors for trading on influence, the Liberal government emphasized in hurt tones that French-Canadians were being singled out — the better to distract voters from the fact that Liberals were being singled out.

Given Canadian regionalism, it is very difficult for national institutions, including national parties, to survive. In 1974, the Progressive Conservative party did have a national economic programme: an immediate wage and price freeze and a later period of controls. Partly for tactical reasons during the campaign, candidates reinterpreted or contradicted the party position. Whatever the benefits to them, the interest of the party as a whole — in having a reputation for reliability or for thoughtfulness about policy options — was undermined. Electoral systems shape parties as institutions directly as well. They make it easier or harder for parties to recruit candidates and to enable candidates to develop political careers. They make it easier or harder for leaders to discipline backbenchers for poor performance. They also encourage or discourage disaffected parliamentarians from leaving their party.

The consequences of all of the above for policy-making should be evident. Cairns suggests that governments are insensitive to the needs of regions not represented strongly in caucus or cabinet (Cairns, 1968, pp. 68-72). Other analysts focus more closely on government formation. An electoral system which made it profitable to multiply parties and appeal to extreme positions might be representative, but would be unable to govern. This is the argument of Ferdinand Hermens (1941) whose powerful attack on proportional electoral systems focussed on the contributions of proportional representation to the rise of Italian and German Fascism. Less dramatically, scholars have asked whether the choice of electoral system affects the ease or difficulty of coalescing social forces, whether agreements will be for a short or long term, and whether agreeing parties will seek to share or to shirk the responsibility of office. On such factors depend whether policy can be made at all and whether it will be moderate or extreme, incremental or wide-ranging.

If these are the issues involved in the choice of electoral system, what are the options? The variants are virtually infinite, but we may focus on five leading cases: the plurality system, alternative vote systems, transferable vote systems, list proportionality systems and a dual representation system. Detailed examples of the translation of votes into parliamentary seats under each system can be found in appendix A.

Very briefly, the plurality system such as now exists in Canada returns one Member of Parliament for each constituency. Parties nominate one candidate (if they nominate any) and the voter indicates his preference by making a mark opposite one name on the ballot. The candidate with the highest number of votes wins.

Under an alternative vote system, voters are encouraged to rank-order the candidates seeking to represent the constituency. Should no candidate get a majority of first preferences, the candidate with the fewest first preferences is dropped and his vote is reallocated among those remaining in the race. This process continues until one candidate has a majority. Part way between this and the plurality system is the French two-ballot system. Again, only one member is returned for each constituency and voters indicate only a single preference. Should no candidate get a majority on the first ballot, a second balloting is held. Weak candidates may be legally obliged to withdraw before the second ballot; conceivably all but the top two candidates could be obliged to withdraw. In France, only very weak candidates are so obliged, and the second ballot is won by the candidate with the highest vote.

Voting on a single transferable vote ballot also requires the rank-ordering of candidates, now in multi-member constituencies. Each party normally nominates more than one candidate but not all parties will have as many contestants as there are seats to be filled. Vote counting is complex but involves establishing an electoral quota — a number of preferences necessary to capture one of the constituency's seats. Surplus votes or votes from low-ranked candidates are redistributed until as many candidates achieve quotas as there are seats to be filled. Seats eventually are allocated roughly proportionately to votes.

List proportional systems also require that constituencies return several members to parliament. Parties nominate lists of candidates, each with as many candidates as there are seats. Depending on the variant, voters may cast a single vote for a list, may cast preference votes for the candidates on a single list, or may distribute preference votes among all listed candidates. In the simplest case of a party vote, counting is simplified. An electoral quota is established, parties get as many seats as they have quotas, and remaining seats are allocated according to specified rules. This system best achieves equivalence between proportion of vote obtained and the proportion of seats won.

A dual representation system is the one to be recommended in the fourth section of this paper, and more detail can be found there. At present, such a system is used in the Federal Republic of Germany. Some of the members of the parliament represent constituencies and are elected by plurality. This part of the system resembles what we have in Canada. German voters simultaneously indicate a party preference on a separate second ballot. That portion of the parliament not sitting for constituencies is allocated among party lists in such a way as to make the overall composition of the parliament reflect party proportions on the ballot of party preferences.

3 The Effects of Electoral Systems

A. Representation of the Electorate

The degree of correlation between the distribution of seats and the distribution of votes is one of the most extensively studied aspects of electoral systems. All plurality systems tend to exaggerate the parliamentary representation of the strongest party, to penalize the second party and to devastate third parties whose strength is thinly spread across the breadth of the country (Rae, 1967, chaps. 4 and 5). In Canada, the NDP and its predecessor, the CCF, have suffered most from this fate. As a regionally concentrated party, (in Quebec since 1962), Social Credit has been treated with relative generosity by the electoral system. This overall success is quite unevenly distributed across the country. Social Credit obtains a surplus of seats in Quebec relative to its vote in that province, but has obtained no seats outside that province since 1968.

Surpluses and shortfalls in the relationship of seats to votes are reported by province in Table 1 for all parties since 1968. These update similar material reported in Cairns (1968, p. 58) and Lovink (1970, p. 510). These more recent data confirm the patterns previously reported for Canada, and are consistent with Douglas Rae's cross-national results cited earlier. With three exceptions concerning the Liberal Party (in Manitoba and the North in 1968 and aggregated nationally in 1972), it is otherwise true that the popular vote leader in any jurisdiction enjoys a bonus of seats, indicated by a ratio larger than 1. This bonus is often quite sizable, amounting to .50 or more. In other words, the party with the most votes may get one-half or two-thirds or even nine-tenths more seats under the present electoral system than it would under a perfectly proportional one. Those parties not topping the polls in any province tend to get less than their proportionate share of seats, although this generalization suffers more exceptions than the previous one. The short-

11

fall is not a function of how far behind any particular party may be. Often third-place finishers do better in translating votes into seats than the second-place party. This has been notably the case for Social Credit in Quebec, finishing third in both 1968 and 1974, but winning more than three times as many seats as the Progressive Conservative party which finished second there. In Manitoba, the NDP has been third in the popular vote throughout the 1968-74 period but has had a more favourable seat-to-vote ratio than the Liberal party at each election.

Table 1 also indicates many severe cases of absolute *non*-representation. The most striking is the Liberal 45% of the electorate in Prince Edward Island in 1968. Not a single Liberal was elected in that province. In terms of voters, the approximately 170,000 Liberals in Alberta, or 25% of the provincial poll, had no partisan representation in either 1972 or 1974. The NDP also managed to win significant proportions of the vote in Alberta since 1968, in Nova Scotia in 1972 and in Newfoundland and New Brunswick in 1974 without electing a member.

Noteworthy also is the volatility of the seat-to-vote ratios, and their inconsistency from province to province. Given the generalizations just reviewed, it is necessarily the case that a party's vote efficiency — the rate at which it translates votes into seats — will increase if it passes the barrier between losing and winning the popular vote contest. The reverse also holds if it loses its standing. The change in Liberal party ratios in New Brunswick and Newfoundland between 1972 and 1974, in British Columbia between 1968 and 1972, and in Ontario from 1968 to 1972 and again, in the opposite direction, from 1972 to 1974 can all be accounted for on this basis. However, it also happens that a party can increase the efficiency of its vote without achieving first place: indeed, it sometimes does so with out even increasing its vote. The Liberals lost votes but gained seats in both Prince Edward Island and Quebec between 1968 and 1972: the NDP did likewise in Nova Scotia between 1972 and 1974. In British Columbia, the Liberals finished third in 1972, second in 1974, but harvested their votes much more efficiently in 1974. The Liberal party finished third in Saskatchewan in all three elections with significantly different seat-to-vote ratios in each.

By inconsistency across provinces, we mean that a party can get approximately the same vote in two different provinces but a much different proportion of seats. In 1968, the Progressive Conservative party got about the same proportion of the vote in New Brunswick as it had in Alberta, and about the same in Ontario as in Manitoba. In each case, they got proportionately fewer seats in the first province mentioned than in the second. Other examples could be given. (There is now a large literature on seat-to-vote ratios. See Sankoff and Mellos, 1973; Tufte, 1973; and Qualter, 1968; and works there cited.)

12

Table 1

The Ratio of Percentage of Seats to Percentage of Votes, Canada and Provinces, 1968-1974

	Lib.	P.C.	NDP	Soc. Cr.	Other
1968 Canada	*1.29**	0.87	0.49	1.21	0.22
Newfoundland	0.32	*1.62*	0/4.4**		0/0.1
Prince Edward Is.	0/45.0	*1.93*	0/3.2		
Nova Scotia	0.24	*1.65*	0/6.7		0/0.1
New Brunswick	1.13	*1.01*	0/4.9	0/0.7	0/0.3
Quebec	*1.41*	0.24	0/7.5	1.15	0/1.1
Ontario	*1.55*	0.59	0.38		1.26
Manitoba	*0.90*	1.23	0.96	0/0.2	0/1.9
Saskatchewan	0.56	*1.03*	1.28		0/0.2
Alberta	0.58	*1.58*	0/9.4		0/4.6
Brit. Columbia	*1.67*	0/19.4	0.91		0/6.1
Yukon-N.W.T.	*0.88*	1.50	0/9.6		
1972 Canada	*0.93*	1.16	0.66	0.75	0.63
Newfoundland	0.96	*1.17*	0/4.7	0/0.2	0/1.3
Prince Edward Is.	0.61	*1.45*	0/7.5	0/0.1	
Nova Scotia	0.26	*1.70*	0/12.3	0/0.3	0/0.1
New Brunswick	1.16	*1.11*	0/5.7	0/5.6	0/0.7
Quebec	*1.54*	0.16	0/6.4	0.83	0.50
Ontario	1.07	*1.16*	0.58	0/0.4	1.26
Manitoba	0.50	*1.48*	0.88	0/0.7	0/0.5
Saskatchewan	0.30	*1.46*	1.07	0/1.8	0/0.1
Alberta	0/25.0	*1.74*	0/12.6	0/4.5	0/0.3
Brit. Columbia	0.60	*1.05*	1.37	0/2.6	0/0.3
Yukon-N.W.T.	0/30.4	*1.28*	1.69		0/1.1
1974 Canada	*1.24*	1.02	0.39	0.82	0.42
Newfoundland	*1.22*	0.98	0/9.5	0/0.1	0/0.1
Prince Edward Is.	0.54	*1.52*	0/4.6		0/0.1
Nova Scotia	0.45	*1.53*	0.81	0/0.4	0/0.1
New Brunswick	*1.27*	0.91	0/8.7	0/2.9	1.23
Quebec	*1.50*	0.19	0/6.6	0.87	0/1.0
Ontario	*1.39*	0.81	0.48	0/0.2	0/0.5
Manitoba	0.56	*1.45*	0.65	0/1.1	0/0.4
Saskatchewan	0.75	*1.69*	0.49	0/1.1	0/0.2
Alberta	0/24.8	*1.63*	0/9.3	0/3.4	0/1.5
Brit. Columbia	1.04	*1.35*	0.38	0/1.2	0/0.5
Yukon-N.W.T.	0/28.1	*1.29*	1.51		

* Italics identifies the party with the highest popular vote in the named jurisdiction.
** An entry in the form "0/x.y" indicates that no seats were won for x.y percent of the vote.

13

In the Canadian context, it is not this capriciousness which is most offensive. The data in Table 1 confirm the persistence of the effect noted earlier by Cairns: the electoral system exaggerates the regionalism of a regionally divided country. Indeed, by giving the Liberals no seats in Alberta and the Progressive Conservatives virtually no seats in Quebec, the electoral system confers a spurious image of unanimity on provinces. By magnifying the success of the provincial vote leader, the electoral system insures that party caucuses will overrepresent any party's "best" province. The consequences of this for the parties and for government policy-making will be explored later in this section.

Would the other electoral systems whose workings we described briefly produce more satisfactory results? Certainly if we consider "satisfactory" to mean a close correspondence between proportion of votes gained and proportion of seats, the German "mixed" system and the other proportional systems, including STV, would be an improvement. Douglas Rae found that all electoral systems exaggerate the seat strength of the leading party to some degree, but the PR systems do so less markedly (Rae, 1967, pp. 70, 88). No system is perfectly evenhanded to all parties, though when a proportional system falls short of perfection it is usually by design. Alternate vote and two-ballot systems do not claim to be proportional systems, only majoritarian ones. Consequently, they are only slightly more benign to minor parties than the plurality system. (See the simulations for Britain in Berrington, 1975). Indeed, seen from the constituency level and depending on rules affecting withdrawal of candidacies in the two-ballot systems, all three systems treat identically any party which achieves less than second place. AV and two-ballot do offer some hope, but no guarantees, to second place finishers. In practice, this hope is occasionally realized. As a result, seat distributions do reflect election results somewhat more closely under these systems than under plurality elections.

So far, representation has been discussed in only a limited sense, that of the correspondence of seat and vote proportions among existing parties. One can broaden the concept to include highly localized minorities or ideological currents not now reflected in any political party.

The problem of ensuring the presence of relatively small minority groups in parliament has not been extensively studied. Jean Laponce's largely formal analysis came to very tentative conclusions. Much depends on the geographic concentration of the minority and its acceptability to the majority (Laponce, 1957). The mechanics of a plurality system are such that, if a group is a local minority, it is only likely to get a nomination by an established party if it can demonstrate such a level of cohesion as to tip the balance and such a level of social acceptability as to lose few votes. Otherwise, too much is at stake for a party to seek its candidate outside the mainstream. Because a metropolitan area is cut up into a number of single member constituencies, any group whose members are scattered through the metropolis finds it difficult to sustain its claim. Though not inherent in the plurality system, gerry-mandering is easier than in systems requiring large multi-member constituencies. By tracing a pen on a map, it is possible to disperse the working class, or the Italians or the X's among a number of constituencies.

Achieving representation for localized minorities poses problems which few electoral systems handle satisfactorily. If we call a local minority "small" when it has fewer members in a constituency than the average second-place vote there, none of the non-proportional systems will afford any guarantees. Nor would the German dual representation system or the various PR systems based on party lists. Whatever the system, the only safeguard for the minority is to be able to trade on its blackmail potential. If a separate minority candidacy could harm at least one of the large parties, that party might be induced to nominate a minority group member as its own candidate. Blackmail potential is only partly a function of the size and discipline of the group in question. It depends, too, on the degree of competition among the established parties. How much competition exists is a highly contingent matter, depending on numbers of contestants and their relative strengths. Only one electoral system clearly does favour localized minorities: the single transferable vote system (Laponce, 1957, pp. 326-8). It is no accident that this system is used in the Republic of Ireland and has been recommended for Northern Ireland (O'Leary, 1975). Under STV, any group that can mobilize $1/(n+1)$ (where "n" is the number of representatives for the multi-member constituency) of the local voters can guarantee itself a seat in Parliament. It is possible to offset or negate the advantage by gerry-mandering or by opting for small constituencies, but STV will achieve representation for localized minorities if that is a goal sought by the community in general.

Previously noted was the Cairns' contention that the present Canadian electoral system submerges a discussion of conflicts in terms of social classes. Social democratic tendencies are not strong in Canada for a variety of historical reasons (Lipset, 1976). As a consequence, the electoral system further weakens political parties trying to appeal to the thin stratum of social democrats scattered through the country. Except in 1958, when the Social Credit party obtained no seats, the CCF/NDP has always had less success in translating votes into seats than has the more sectional Social Credit party. The national figures in Table 1 simply prolong the trends charted in Cairns' Table II. These hold despite (perhaps "because" of) the fact that the CCF/NDP has been the third largest party in Canada since 1935. A social democratic appeal is inherently a nationalizing one, and the party has stuck to it, despite the contrary incentives provided by the electoral system. Within certain provinces — Saskatchewan and British Columbia in particular — the NDP does benefit from the workings of the plurality system. It is testimony to the commitment of party activists to its ideology that it has resisted the temptation to become a "Western Canada" party or an anti-French party.

The major partisan beneficiary of a more proportional electoral system in Canada would be the NDP. Without changing its vote at all, it would approximately double its representation in the federal parliament. Whatever one's own ideological leanings, this additional parliamentary strength might be seen as desirable as a vehicle for changing the manner in which problems in Canada are defined. At the same time, however, every reader will be able to supply a list of ideologies to which he would prefer to *deny* representation. The fact that proportional representation systems make it easier for new parties to form is one of the major arguments used against them. We must ask whether it is true that the plurality system in Canada excludes overtly racist (anti-French, anti-Semitic, anti-coloured) candidates. Does it exclude those of the far left or the far right? If the answer is "yes", is it a desirable consequence?

It is obvious that no electoral system will exclude dominant tendencies. To say that a plurality electoral system encourages centrist tendencies, one must first assume that the electorate itself is concentrated in the center. If that is the case, and given that so much turns on coming in first under a plurality system, one is led to the conclusion that parties will not stray far from the center. This argument rests on two doubtful assumptions, however. The first is that all voters, wherever they may be located in an issue space, are equally likely to change their vote consequent on a change in appeals by party leaders. The second is that the model applies to a single constituency, or that the whole country is treated as one constituency.

Abandoning the second assumption raises the possibility that the incentives of particular candidates are different from those of the national parties. The center of voter opinion for the nation as a whole is unlikely to coincide with the center of opinion in every constituency (Robertson, 1976, pp. 49-54). This proposition may be taken as axiomatic in a regionally divided country such as Canada. The courage of a Robert Stanfield in repudiating a Leonard Jones is not matched by most party leaders, though fortunately not many vitriolic racists have yet emerged as credible candidates in Canada. Any opinion, extreme or moderate, will find representation under a plurality electoral system if its strength is concentrated strategically in some constituencies. The interplay of party size, vote concentration and representation under plurality rules has been elegantly demonstrated for Canada by Richard Johnston and Janet Ballantyne (1977).

This evidence does not address the contention that party leaders, as opposed to individual candidates, must search out center opinion if they are to win parliamentary majorities. It follows from the first assumption that a party leader inclined to appeal to "extreme" voters (those farthest from the center of national opinion) would lose more votes in the center than he might hope to gain on the fringes. The Goldwater and McGovern candidacies in the United States are cited as evidence that the first assumption holds. Despite this, it is not difficult to find counter examples of national politicians using the code words of extremist opinion. Moreover, voting surveys in many countries have confirmed the existence of substantial numbers of voters who are either so solidly committed to one political party or who are so disinterested in things political as to be virtually immune to appeals of politicians (Converse, 1962; Leduc et al, 1976). This frees the party leader to flirt with extremist groups. Even if compelled to do so in ambiguous terms so as not to bestir his faithful support, the cues might be sufficient to attract the more extreme groups. As they have, we assume, no political champion, they might move in unison to the most subtle of rhythms which might pass unheard by traditional party supporters. One can welcome the fact that the National Front in Britain is such a small party. Yet one must raise the question, if Britain had an electoral system which provided incentives to the National Front to marshall every bit of its vote, would the Thatcher Conservative Party put the issue of immigration on the political agenda? With the National Front in Parliament, other parties would be less able to attract votes from the political extremes. It might therefore be preferable to have racist parties free to compete under an electoral system that enables them to maximize their parliamentary representation. Clearly this would not be so if the non-racist alternatives could win less than two-thirds of the parliamentary seats. The racists would then dominate the opposition with unfortunate long-run consequences (Hermens, 1941, pp. 27, 28; Sartori, 1966, pp. 137-176). However, it is unlikely that any electoral system could block so strong a movement. So long as the extremists remain numerically weak, they will be ignored as possible partners both by the governing and by the constitutional opposition parties. This, in essence, is what happens in Italy where both the neo-fascist/monarchist *Destra Nazionale* and the left splinters from the Communist Party are present in parliament but largely excluded from governmental politics. We need be under no illusion that parliamentary representation somehow "tames" the extremist parties. To return to the

Italian example, the excluded parties do sit in Parliament but also engage in street violence. The justification for representing *them* is that moderate parties are forced to greater effort to mobilize their own support.

As the example of the British Conservatives and the immigration issue suggests, the supposed discipline of the plurality system in forcing parties to seek the centre is attenuated if one's most faithful voters are themselves centrists rather than extremists. While those who wish to burst into the system, as Hitler did, must find substantial concentrations of extremist voters, parties that are already in the system must appeal to the *most volatile* voters. These may be the ones who hold extreme opinions. Opportunist party leaders will not even insist that volatile voters be territorially concentrated since they can rely on the party faithful to provide some territorial presence.

It is also true that, whatever the logic of competition under a plurality electoral system, the outcomes of plurality elections can be quite capricious. We have already seen examples of this. Duff Spafford has shown more systematically that the seat shares of major parties in Canada depend most decisively, as one would hope, on their own share of the vote (Spafford, 1970). However, it also depends, to a not negligible extent, on the number of candidates put up by minor parties. With a vote highly divided among several candidates, the plurality electoral system is unable to exclude extremist candidates.

The fact remains, however, that small extremist groups only gain representation under plurality electoral systems under unusual conditions, but would much more readily find seats under most proportional representation systems. Opponents of PR deny that there is any advantage in representing extremist political movements in parliament. F.A. Hermens' classic attack argues that many extremist movements are largely ephemeral, or would be so but for the benefits they can draw from PR systems. Under such systems, movements gain representation in parliament and credibility as contestants in elections. They remain as available and plausible alternatives if regimes run into economic difficulties, and may be able to make difficult the functioning of a democratic regime (Hermens, 1941, chaps. 2 and 3, esp. pp. 25-27). In the light of hindsight, it no longer seems plausible to argue that the Fascists in Italy and Germany after 1919 were artificially sustained by the electoral system. No more persuasive is the subsidiary proposition that their exclusion from parliament (which might have been achieved by some electoral systems) would have meant their exclusion from political life.

Hermens' criticism of proportional representation was much more fundamental than this, however. He denied, as a general proposition, that political interests, at least those that are primarily ideological, have any existence independent of the electoral system. There is nothing "out there" to represent (Hermens, 1941, pp. 13-14). Rather, political group-ings are created as a by-product of the manoeuvering of political actors and these reflect, at least in part, the incentives provided by the electoral system. Attempting to decide what is "real" is one of the least promising and most inconclusive detours in social argument. Canadian experience does confirm the effect insofar as the NDP is concerned, but one might be tempted to argue that the social democratic tendency in Canada is the more "real" because of its ability to survive the disincentives of the electoral system. The faithfulness of NDP supporters who have no realis-tic hope of electing a candidate is a source of strength in the current party system and evidence that traditional parties are unlikely to be swept away by new parties of protest as soon as barriers to parliamentary representation are lowered.

Fortunately, one can sidestep the Hermens question in the Canadian case. The main interests to be represented are regional and linguistic groups. These are more fixed in size and more clearly defined than are ideological preferences. They certainly have a long history and cannot be considered as artifacts – though they may, as Cairns has argued, have been overemphasized in Canadian politics. It is still important to ask, however, which French Canadian, or Prairie or British Columbia or Maritime interest is to be represented. Opponents of PR argue that, even if these groups have relatively fixed boundaries, the definition of their interest would undergo a progressive radicalization under a system of proportional representation. Within each group, the present moderate parties would be challenged by more intransigent ones, given an elec-toral system which reduced barriers to entry (Hermens, 1941, pp. 15-30; more recently, others have proposed a similar model for the time path of ethnic politics and these authors do not assume any particular electoral system: Rabushka and Shepsle, 1972, pp. 62-92).

Such a scenario ignores a very important effect of PR systems: the virtual impossibility of capturing one hundred percent of the seats allo-cated to any regional or linguistic community. In another context, Her-mens makes this very point when he complains that PR exaggerates individualism and destroys community. It frees the voter from having to decide which of several candidates would be the best spokesmen for the local community, discounting the candidate's programme by the chances of his being elected. PR, instead, enables the voter to define his own constituency. Social democrats in eastern Ontario would not have to choose between the Liberal and the Progressive Conservative parties to get the best representation for their area but could identify themselves with the social democratic "constituency" of Ontario, and vote NDP (Hermens, 1941, pp. 78-85). This very fact makes it unlikely, at least in the absence of extremely bitter conflict, that the moderate elements in

19

any regional or linguistic community could be totally defeated. In a later subsection, we shall examine in more detail the nature of voter support for the present parties in order to assess their staying power.

Moreover, the parliamentary system has its own centripetal logic. If the Canadian party system were to fragment, with many new parties joining the existing ones in Parliament, many alternative governing coalitions would be possible. Virtually all, simply by the mathematics of the situation, would have to contain representation from all regions. Each contender for regional spokesmanship would have an incentive to moderate his position in order to become "ministrable". Giovanni Sartori was the first to draw our attention to the unfortunate consequences of "polarized pluralism", but he never established a one-to-one correlation between the electoral system and that condition. The more important variable seems to be ideological distance and its embodiment in an "anti-system" party (Sartori, 1966 and *idem.* 1976). While there is certainly neither proof nor divine promise that Canada could never produce a paralysis-inducing anti-system party, the ideological tradition does not make that a likely development. While Canadian national identity is weak, the socialization of Canadians into the North American ideological style seems quite widespread and secure. Moreover, Canada enjoys a much longer popular partisan history than did Germany or Italy immediately after the First World War.

It is possible to set fairly precise limits on the extent to which any electoral system will facilitate the emergence of new parties or the fragmentation of existing ones. Rae, Hanby and Loosemore (1971) define and measure two concepts: the threshold of exclusion and the threshold of representation. The first asks: how many votes would a party require to assure itself of a seat, given that votes for its opponents were distributed as unfavourably as possible to its own interests? The second measures the opposite: if opponents' votes were distributed as favourably as possible to the interests of party A, how small a share of the vote would A need to get a seat? In other than two-party systems, the threshold of exclusion is higher than the threshold of representation, no matter what the electoral system used. Table 2 below is drawn from Rae, Hanby and Loosemore (1971, p. 485) and from Lijphart and Gibberd (1977) whose correction of the former authors' calculations on some points is persuasive (1977, p. 225).

Analysis of these formulae suggest the following conclusions:

1. the threshold of exclusion is higher in a plurality than in any PR system, whatever its specific rule for allocating seats;
2. the threshold of exclusion is identical for all PR systems so long as the number of parties exceeds the number of seats;

Table 2

Threshold of Exclusion and Representation for Different Types* of Electoral System

	Plurality	d'Hondt	St. Laguë	Modified St. Laguë	Largest Remainder
Threshold of Exclusion if:					
n-1 GE m**	1/2	$1/(m+1)$	$1/(m+1)$	$1/(m+1)$	$1/(m+1)$
m/2 GE n-1 GE m	N/A***	$1/(m+1)$	$1/(2m-n+2)$	$1.4/(1.6m-.2n+1.6)$	$(n-1)/mn$
n-1 GE m/2	N/A***	$1/(+1)$	$1/(m-n+2)$	$1.4/(2m-n+2.4)$	$(n-1)\ mn$
Threshold of Representation	1/n	$1/(m+n-1)$	$1/(2m+n-2)$	$1.4/(2m+1.4n-2.4)$	$1/mn$

* The types other than "Plurality" are various seat allocation systems used under proportional representation systems and are defined precisely in Appendix A.

** n is the number of parties contesting a constituency
   GE means "greater than or equal to"
   m is the number of seats for a constituency

*** Under a plurality system, the number of seats is almost always 1. We assume a democracy with more than one party; hence the non-applicability.

3. where there are fewer parties than constituency seats, the d'Hondt system has the highest threshold of exclusion of any PR system (descriptions of various types of electoral systems can be found in Appendix A);
4. the threshold of representation is highest for plurality electoral systems, higher for the d'Hondt system than for any other PR system, and lowest for largest remainder systems;
5. in PR systems, the number of seats being contested may offset the effects of counting rules: the more seats returned from any constituency, the lower the thresholds;
6. for St. Lagüe and Largest Remainder systems, thresholds of exclusion increase as the number of parties increases up to the point where the number of parties exceeds the number of seats by 1. Given large constituencies and relatively few parties initially, it becames progressively harder for additional parties to enter the system.

These generalizations confirm the conventional wisdom about electoral systems, but only up to a point. Even putting aside the causal connection between electoral systems and numbers of parties, and speaking only of "facilitation", it is clear that this "facilitation" is not infinite. District magnitude — the number of seats from each constituency — is an independent facilitating factor. It is therefore possible to engineer limits to the degree to which any electoral system will reward the political organization of currents of opinion. The precise rule chosen to allocate the seats will also affect the degree of facilitation afforded to the emergence of new parties.

B. Responsiveness to the Electorate

There are two things at issue here. First, to what extent does the voter feel he can change things through the use of his vote? Is the system sensitive to changes in the behaviour of any voter? Secondly, to what extent does the voter's possession of the vote make the politicians see him as a person worth courting? In fact the questions are closely related, since if the vote cannot affect anything, it is probably not worth having. In practice the two questions are separable, and answers depend on the level of political activity being examined. We might be talking about constituency politics or parliamentary politics.

Turning to the question of the "leverage" of a vote, we might ask whether or not a vote has impact independently of the immediately local circumstances where it is cast. We have seen that this is not true in any electoral system. Thresholds of representation are always lower, depending on the number of candidates among whom the vote is divided and on the pattern of the division. Proportional systems are applied to much bigger constituencies, however, and so dilute the impact of local circumstances. The larger district magnitudes and the lesser thresholds make it more likely that a voter will see his vote as having contributed to the election of some representative from his most preferred party. Under PR, voters are more likely to feel it possible to vote "sincerely". With a plurality electoral system, voters whose own candidate is far from victory and where there are two other candidates relatively evenly matched face a dilemma. Should they vote for their most preferred candidate or against their least preferred candidate? (Spafford, 1972; Spafford, 1974).

To speak of a voter being efficacious in any realistic sense may strike readers as curiously idealistic or romantic (Barry, 1970, pp. 13-19). In 1974, 9.67 million people voted in Canada. The smallest constituency had 13,952 eligible voters, but 90% of all constituencies had at least 33,000 eligible voters. How can one voter against so many change a member of parliament, much less a government? Probably voters do not calculate their potential efficacy in quite that way; certainly parties do not. Voter efficacy is primarily a question of the MP's margin of victory. Between 1953 and 1972, a Member of Parliament who had won the previous election with a margin over his nearest opponent of no more than 10% of the total vote had on average only a 50:50 chance of retaining his seat (Lovink, 1973, p. 374). In such a circumstance, it is likely that both he and his opponent will be assiduous in courting the voter. A small shift in vote can lead to a large shift in seat proportions (Rae, 1967, table 5.2; and Tufte, 1973) and, in an individual case, can mean the difference between victory and defeat.

However, a legislator's job security varies exponentially with his margin of victory. In federal elections in Canada since 1953 the odds for re-election have usually been 3:1 where margin of victory had been between 10 and 20%, and nearer to 9:1 above such margins (Lovink, 1973, p. 374). Here again, then, the plurality system seems to be one whose benefits are spatially delimited. Of course, it is not entirely the fault of the electoral system that some constituencies are more competitive than others. At crucial turning points in our political history, parties have had to choose policies favourable to one region or another. The alienation of Quebec by the Conservative party in 1917 was but the end point of a series of decisions which angered French-speaking Catholics. Similarly, there is a widespread feeling in the Canadian West that the region is exploited for the benefit of Ontario and Quebec. At different times, one or the other and occasionally both major Canadian parties have been seen as the political expression of that exploitation. Currently the Liberal party is so viewed and it is not difficult to find foundation for this. While we shall return to the point in discussing parties as institutions, we should note here Professor Cairns' argument that the plurality electoral system leads parties to compound the effects of their past choices (Cairns, 1968, pp. 68-72). A party having alienated some region sets in motion a train of events, making it more likely that the party will reinforce that alienation and less likely that the party will move dramatically to especially favour its weak region. However one might wish to regard the specific role of the electoral system in affecting the degree of competitiveness in constituencies, it is clear that plurality voting *defines* competitiveness in a restrictive way: essentially, by reference to the margin of votes separating the two most popular opponents. By contrast, the reference point for Alternative Vote systems is the gap between any party's first count vote and the 50% point. Therefore, in systems of alternative voting, either of the one-ballot or the French two-ballot variety, second place is almost as important an achievement as first place (provided that the latter does not equal 50 percent of first preferences). Under these counting rules, all competitors have considerable incentive to maximize the number and discipline of their voters. Even parties clearly unable to finish first or second will attempt to obtain, and later deliver, blocks of votes to leading contenders in order to bargain for concessions. Consequently constituencies with, for example, a 45:30:15:10 vote distribution among 4 parties will be much more hotly contested under AV than under a plurality electoral system. The incentive for party activity, and hence the effect of the ballot, is less in Alternative Vote systems where first-count victories are achieved with more than 50% of the vote. Even here, however, the fact that small parties could have importance if the votes of the leader were to require a second count may provide some incentive to maximize the size of the active electorate. Though comparable studies are not available for non-plurality systems, recent studies show that turnout declines as margin of victory increases in plurality electoral systems (Irvine, 1976: Denver and Hands, 1974; Kim, Petrocik and Enokson, 1975). This may indicate the voter's estimate of the degree of responsiveness to his vote.

Systems of list proportionality may not be much better with regard to encouraging responsiveness to voters. Parliamentarians at the very top of their respective party lists are virtually guaranteed re-election. They may, for reasons of party unity, come actively to the support of their more precariously placed colleagues or attempt to increase their parliamentary numbers. The incentives to do so are not strong, however, except for parties which are systematically excluded from government. For them, an increasing vote may lead to increasing recognition and consultation. Those parties which are usually included in government coalitions are so at least as much because of their position in the parliamentary ideological spectrum as for any claim based on their size. The Communist Party in Italy, by contrast, has every incentive to work to increase its vote and has done so continuously since the war. It has been able to use its success to edge closer and closer to some share of government power.

In terms of giving voters leverage over representatives, PR/STV is probably the most important. Every constituency in Canada, no matter how one-sided it now appears, could return at least one representative whose position was precarious. Indeed, in a five-member constituency where three parties managed to elect representatives (a not unlikely occurrence in Canada outside the Atlantic provinces) each party would have at least one member whose seat was marginal.

It could be argued that the voter's interest is less in his ability to change parliamentary representatives, who tend to become party ciphers in any event, as in his ability to change governments. Given the tendency of plurality systems to exaggerate the effects of voter swing, governments are probably most vulnerable in a plurality system. In a proportional system, the effects of vote swing are less impressive and the identity of the main governing parties changes only imperceptibly, if at all. That this relative invulnerability exists, there can be no question. Whether it makes PR elections seem more ritualistic to the voters is more debatable. Certainly, voter turnout in PR systems tends to be higher than in plurality systems. During the 1960's, both seemed equally susceptible to the rapid emergence of "flash" parties which opposed the whole existing party spectrum and were able to strike a responsive chord in some segments of the electorate. On balance, however, it does seem that plurality systems make it easier for the voter to bring about a qualitative, but probably not a radical, change in the way he is governed. In Quebec in 1976, the change was substantial. As we shall see in a later discussion, the policy-making perspective differs from the voter responsiveness perspective in evaluating this tendency of plurality systems.

Wilfrid Dewachter has observed that a key issue affecting political power is the question of who will be in the cabinet (Dewachter, 1978). It is probable that no system for electing representatives is decisive in this respect. By constitutional convention, the plurality electoral system in Canada or Britain does have a negative influence. A person who cannot win a constituency cannot be in a cabinet, of the real or shadow variety. There are well-known cases of such veto in Canadian politics: Arthur Meighen in 1943, General McNaughton in 1944, Pierre Juneau in 1976, John Evans in 1978. There are no doubt many other cases where defeat is a by-product of other voter decisions, rather than an active veto. Insofar as proportional systems produce parliamentary configurations that require a coalition government, cabinet bargaining becomes a much more public process than it is in Canada or Britain. It may disperse influence beyond the parliamentary parties to the executives of party organizations, but probably not so far as to give more influence to voters. All coalitions are ultimately responsible to an electorate which may react negatively if important interests are excluded from a cabinet, but this is no more true of multi-party than of intra-party coalitions.

Systems of proportional representation involving the allocation of parliamentary seats to party lists are criticized by Hermens as leading to the weakening and stagnation of the political elite (Hermens, 1941, pp. 51-66). Those at the top of the list have no incentive to maximize the vote for their party; their election is assured, barring total collapse of the party. They *do* have an incentive to keep their top spot and not yield it to a younger man. Younger men placed at the bottom of party lists will find little reward for whatever effort they expend and will cease to campaign vigourously. In Hermens' view, campaign effort must decline: it is either unnecessary or unrewarded. Young people will find aging parties, and alienated people will find that nothing changes and will reject electoral battle as a means of political activity. Before a political elite can stagnate, it must first exist. The more pressing problem in Canada may be to develop a cadre of experienced parliamentarians. J.A.A. Lovink has examined the years of consecutive parliamentary experience of Canadian MPs from 1925 to 1972. The median number of years of prior experience has not exceeded 5 in that period and has not exceeded 4 since 1973 (Lovink, 1973, p. 369). In other words, after any election, approximately half the parliamentarians will have had less than one term's experience.

Table 3

Executive and Legislative Experience of Canadian Cabinet Ministers

	Dec., 1956	*Dec., 1962*	*April, 1977*
Median months in same portfolio	74	28	8
Median months in cabinet	93	54	53
Median months in parliament before first appointment to cabinet	23	72	61
Percent appointed to cabinet before sitting in parliament	39%	4%	0
Median months in parliament	138	126	117
Number of ministers*	18	24	31

* Includes the Prime Minister.

SOURCE: *Canadian Parliamentary Guide.*

Table 3 examines the parliamentary and cabinet experience of members of the St. Laurent, Diefenbaker and Trudeau cabinets. In appraising these figures, it must be kept in mind that the St. Laurent Liberals were coming to the end of a term which had begun in 1935, that the Diefenbaker government had only been in power for 54 months, and that the Liberals had resumed office in 1963. Almost two-fifths of the 1956 cabinet had been first named to the government and later returned to parliament in bye-elections. The median cabinet member waited less than two years on the benches before appointment. While most members of that St. Laurent cabinet had little political experience before joining the government, they were able to accumulate a great deal of it after appointment. By 1956, the median cabinet member had sat in parliament for 138 months, over 11.5 years, and had almost eight years of cabinet experience, virtually all of it in the same portfolio. The median cabinet minister had been heading the same department for more than six years. The Diefenbaker cabinet of 1961 had not had as much opportunity to accumulate executive experience, but had almost as long a parliamentary experience — over ten years — as the Liberal cabinet had had. Over half the members of the cabinet had been there since the beginning and had served the full 54 months, while the median member had waited six years before getting into the cabinet. Many of those years, clearly, were spent in opposition. New appointments and cabinet shuffles meant that the median cabinet minister had had only 28 months in the same portfolio by December, 1961. The Trudeau cabinet, in April 1977, had the least executive experience. The median cabinet minister had been in parliament for a little less than the Prime Minister. The median member had had to wait five years as a backbencher before appointment to the cabinet. This was less than the Diefenbaker appointees but considerably more than the St. Laurent ministers. None of the members of the Trudeau cabinet was brought into office by bye-election, though Table 3 does not capture the unsuccessful attempt to so appoint Pierre Juneau.

Does all of this constitute a political elite? The relatively short parliamentary apprenticeship before joining the cabinet indicates that it is not. Half the cabinet had faced the electorate only twice before appointment to the cabinet — only slightly more experience than Lovink found for the median MP. The fact of Liberal dominance in Canada provides more opportunity for long cabinet experience, but this is not reflected in the Trudeau cabinet. Both the Diefenbaker and Trudeau cabinets contained members with less than five years cabinet experience and very little experience in managing a specific department. The St. Laurent cabinet had been much superior in that respect. Although the median member has had upwards of ten years legislative experience in each case, this experience is very unequally distributed between members coming from a party's most favoured regions, and those from its least favoured regions. Of the Quebec members of the Diefenbaker cabinet, Balcer had been in parliament since 1949, and William Hamilton since 1953, but the others, O'Hurley, Dorion, Sevigny and Flynn, had been elected only in 1957 or 1958. Of the Western representatives in the Trudeau cabinet in April, 1977, all but Ron Basford had been first elected to parliament in 1968, and only Basford and Lang had been in the cabinet since at least 1968. Marchand, Campagnolo and Guay had had less than one year of cabinet experience in April, 1977. If Canadian political parties had more elaborate research or other organizational wings, it might be possible to compensate for the lack of parliamentary experience. It is, indeed, the case that some people come into the parliament and the cabinet after having spent time as a ministerial assistant. However, this route is unavailable to opposition parties who therefore have few opportunities to groom members of their future leadership from regions where the party is electorally unsuccessful.

To conclude this sub-section of our evaluation of electoral systems, we may note two counts on which plurality systems are said to be preferable to other systems of representation. One is the relative simplicity of the voting and counting procedure. On average, the voter in any system using single member constituencies has fewer candidates to keep in view than voters in multi-member constituencies. While this is true, it is not a necessary feature of the electoral system. Nor is it particularly significant. Whether many names are included on a list, or whether a single name is identified with a political party, as in Canada, it is the party label that is the major landmark on the ballot (Kamin, 1958). Regardless of the number of candidates, it is the number of parties that determines the amount of information most voters need and use in casting their vote.

In electoral systems based on alternative or transferable voting, the voter must keep in mind, and develop a strategy for dealing with, many names on a ballot under different party labels. Here again, parties have considerable incentive to "educate" their electorate to the proper strategy and may be seen to take over much of the burden of decision-making. (Carty, forthcoming). Despite party effort, such forms of ballot do show a tendency for elections to turn on irrelevant features of a constituency situation. In both Ireland and in local elections in the United States, candidates whose surnames begin with letters at the beginning of the alphabet seem to be favoured (Robson and Walsh, 1974; Bain and Hecock, 1957; Taebel, 1975). This could be corrected by randomizing the order of names on ballot papers. Problems of strategic voting also arise in plurality electoral systems, as we have seen, and here parties are less good guides to action, since all seek to maximize their own vote and are loath to admit to not being in contention.

Finally, it is argued that a plurality electoral system or, more precisely, a system of single-member constituencies, is preferable in cementing the link between constituent and representative. An exhaustive discussion of this contention can be found in Crewe (1975). Very briefly, he finds that the impact of a member of parliament on his constituency in Britain is not as extensive as has been assumed, and does not obviously vary by constituency size. He also suggests that, insofar as the attentiveness of representative to constituents' views and needs is a function of electoral incentives more than of personal inclination, the greater vulnerability of MPs in a system like PR/STV would enhance the link between representative and represented. So would the need, in such an electoral system, for MPs to differentiate themselves from other candidates of their own party as well as from those of other parties. List systems do not reward constituency service in this way.

C. Organization *for* the Electorate

The title of this subsection seems curious in the light of liberal democratic theory which celebrates the virtue of the independent citizen deliberating on the best way to achieve the public good. The argument here is that democracy needs strong political parties. Their importance does not primarily arise from their capacity to discover what citizens want. Survey research could do that better. Rather, parties are necessary as agencies to mobilize popular power to obtain what people want or need. For a variety of reasons, parties in Canada, and perhaps in all industrial democracies, fail to live up fully to their potential. While it would take us too far afield to explore all the reasons, the type of electoral system in each country seems to be a potent influence on the organizational capacity of political parties. For parties to be strong instruments for popular government, they must exhibit at least the following four characteristics:

1. a secure base of support;
2. committed activists and parliamentarians;
3. sensitivity to popular feelings and needs;
4. a knowledge of where they want to go and, in general terms at least, of how to get there.

A party with a secure base of support operates in a more predictable environment than one which does not know where its next vote is coming from. It is therefore more likely to pursue a consistent line of policy and to adapt to, rather than collapse before, changing circumstances. It will be less subject to blackmail by those who control money, or media, or purport to have better information about the needs of social groups than the parties do themselves. In order to achieve such security, the party must conceive itself, and be viewed, as the spokesman for a specific group or ideal. Often such parties will have organizational interlocks with other agencies representing the same bloc. Parties strong in this sense are less and less common. Given the multiplication of wants and the fragmentation of groups inherent in industrial society, it is difficult to discover groups or ideals that both evoke longterm commitment and are large enough to approach being half the electorate. As a result, major parties in Canada have usually tried to appeal to everyone by focussing on matters with which no one can disagree: honesty and competence in government, and economic growth. Where they do get into themes which might evoke a conflict of interest — frugality in government now replacing generosity towards those who could not provide for themselves, or greater or lesser bilingualism in government institutions — the major parties rarely disagree but manage to change their past commitments, if not in unison, at least in a race to get to the same point, as witness the 1974 disagreement over wage and price controls or the 1978 disagreement over income tax deductions for homeowners. Even these differences are not rooted in any distinct and continuing party interests. A party which purports to be everyone's instrument is nobody's instrument, and nobody need feel any loyalty to it. This, of course, is an exaggeration of the Canadian situation, as we see in Table 4, drawn from the 1974 election survey (Clarke et al, 1979). There is some social differentiation and there are many loyal partisans in Canada. Comparison with other countries is difficult since comparable measurement does not exist for many countries. Reports of the degree of attachment to political parties indicate that loyalties are more widespread in Britain and Australia than in Canada (Irvine, 1975). It also appears to be the case that the impact of party attachment on stabilizing the party vote is less in Canada than in the United States or Austraila (Elkins, 1978; Irvine and Gold, 1979). As these observations suggest, party loyalty in Canada rests on a weak foundation — weak both from the point of view of the voter and that of the party. It is more often derivative from family tradition than based on political interests. In Canada, party divides Canadians along the lines of 19th century conflicts rather than orienting the electorate to the solution of current issues. The existence of party loyalty devoid of current policy content may benefit parties by leaving them free to adopt any position they wish on current issues. But this very freedom robs a party of its character, and the concomitantly weak social roots of parties make them more susceptible to pressure from small groups.

Table 4

Indicators of Popular Attachment to Federal Political Parties by Region, 1974
(Numbers in brackets are the base for the percentage)

	Atlantic	Quebec	Ontario	Prairies	B.C.
1974 Liberals Voters					
% Lib. in 1972	74 (91)	81 (335)	68 (376)	72 (95)	63 (73)
% "Always voted Lib."	70 (92)	66 (331)	55 (370)	56 (99)	51 (73)
% "Very strong" or "fairly strong" Lib. ID.	82 (92)	83 (355)	73 (376)	57 (99)	66 (73)
% Seeing party diff.*	76 (93)	83 (336)	83 (383)	86 (100)	92 (75)
1974 P.C. Voters					
% PC in 1972	80 (66)	44 (55)	70 (234)	63 (131)	44 (79)
% "Always voted PC"	63 (65)	34 (53)	47 (236)	44 (133)	28 (81)
% "Very strong" or "fairly strong" PC ID.	64 (66)	44 (55)	57 (236)	59 (133)	46 (81)
% Seeing party diff.*	77 (67)	80 (56)	80 (238)	85 (134)	87 (83)
*1974 Third Party Voters***					
% Same in 1972	48 (10)	66 (55)	68 (104)	68 (37)	72 (40)
% "Always voted" same	23 (11)	48 (54)	49 (103)	46 (39)	48 (44)
% "Very strong" or "fairly strong" party ID.	72 (11)	58 (55)	71 (104)	62 (39)	57 (44)
% Seeing party diff.*	86 (11)	62 (55)	81 (104)	77 (39)	84 (44)
% of voters*** who changed their vote between '72 and '74	33 (189)	44 (607)	38 (795)	44 (315)	49 (221)
% of respondents claiming to have voted for different parties over time	40 (212)	50 (679)	51 (856)	54 (389)	61 (246)
% of sample with weak or no party identification	29 (220)	34 (702)	31 (878)	42 (393)	41 (252)
% of respondents who say it makes no difference which party forms the gov't.	18 (216)	25 (691)	20 (875)	18 (391)	10 (251)

* Those who say it makes "a great deal of difference" or "some difference" which party forms the federal government.
** Social Credit in Quebec, NDP elsewhere.
*** all who voted in 1972 or 1974 or both.

Table 4 provides some indicators of the political orientations held by members of the most important voting coalitions in 1974. Those who voted Liberal in that year were relatively strongly attached to that party, although the precise degree of attachment depended on the region of residence. The 1974 election represented a resurgence of Liberal fortunes by comparison to 1972 and one would expect that the 1974 Liberals would include a good number who had not supported the party before. The figures in the first line of Table 4 cannot be explained entirely this way, however. The 1972 Liberal vote in Ontario or B.C. was more than 80% as large as the 1974 vote, but only about two-thirds claim consistency. The rest are more volatile voters moving in ways apparently unrelated to aggregate trends. The same holds for the three-quarters repeat Liberal voters in the Atlantic region and the Prairies or the 80 percent in Quebec who claim to have twice voted Liberal. The Liberals actually had more votes on the Prairies in 1972 than they had in 1974. Turning to the second line of the table, west of Quebec only half the 1974 Liberal voters claim undying fidelity to that party; east of the Ottawa River, about three-quarters do. A similar east to west differentiation is found in party identification. Sentiments of identification are weakest in the Prairies and B.C. and strongest in the east. A reverse pattern holds for the sentiment that the party in government matters, but in general high proportions of voters feel that it makes some difference which party is in office. This may be a consequence of the marked party differences over wage and price controls in 1974.

The Progressive Conservative coalition is weaker, and the weakness shows up most particularly in Quebec and B.C. where the party is weakest organizationally. Though again, PC voters do sense that party differences are important, their behaviour does suggest that the party is seen as an omnibus which one gets on and off at will. Even third party voters are as strongly or more strongly attached to their parties as Progressive Conservative voters. Only in the Atlantic region does that party seem strongly rooted. Still, this may be a pessimistic reading of the table. At least one-third of Quebec Conservatives claim to have stayed with the party through its leanest years. This is the base on which the party could build under a new electoral system and on which it could rely in the face of threats from new competitors. Others of the presently established parties have similar or stronger bases, even in their weakest regions. The last four lines of Table 4 indicate that, while less than 20% (25% in Quebec) feel that the present system offers no effective choice, between thirty and forty percent feel no psychological attachment to current competitors and about half have switched their votes among the competitors. Indeed, between one-third and one-half claim to have voted differently (by switching or abstaining once) over a two year period.

Clearly, Canada's is not the strongest party system to which to suddenly reduce the entry barriers; the more so since one must discount present evidence of fidelity as predictive of behaviour faced with a wider set of parties. Under a new electoral system the race between present parties strengthening their hold on their electorates and new parties trying to attract support would by no means be pre-determined. Still, established parties would be in the best position to take advantage of the possibilities of the new electoral system, particularly as they control the timing of the introduction of that system.

A move to greater proportionality in Canada would mean that no area of the country could be considered safe. Liberals would find that they had to compete for the Quebec vote both against currently existing Canadian parties, and possibly against new parties as well. It would have to extend its organization in Quebec and probably have to decide *which* Quebeckers it would attempt to mobilize. By no longer being able to make the diffuse claim outside Quebec that *it* was the only party able to get support in Quebec, the Liberals would also have to develop much more specific appeals for English Canada as well. Eventually, one might expect these more focussed appeals to be supplemented with organizational ties.

As to the second criterion of organizational strength, one may posit that activists and parliamentarians will only be committed to a party if it is worth their while, with "worth" probably most saliently defined in career terms. Party and parliamentary work must be seen as leading to positions of power that could not otherwise be obtained outside the party. We have already seen that less than half of Canadian parliamentarians ever get the opportunity to develop political careers and that, in terms of experience before first appointment to cabinet, parliamentary experience is not particularly rewarded in any case (See also Meisel, 1963; Meisel 1978). Dedication to political life is even less in evidence among defeated candidates. Table 5 examines the recent experience of defeated major party candidates in two regions where the effects of the electoral system are particularly strong, and one where the parties are more competitive. In fact, the weakness of political competition seems unrelated to careerism. Losing candidates generally do not contest subsequent elections. There may be some tendency to try again when elections follow closely one on the other as in 1972-74. Further study would be needed to see if this is peculiar to those elections. While the lack of political dedication cuts across areas of political advantage or disadvantage, its effects are most pernicious in the areas where parties fail to elect many representatives to parliament. Among the Progressive Conservative candidates in Quebec who lost in 1968 and did not try again were Marcel Faribault, Julien Chouinard, and Paul Beaulieu, plus a number of

Table 5

Proportion of Unsuccessful Major Party Candidates Who Contest Subsequent Elections Quebec, Prairies, Ontario - 1968-74

	Lost 1968 Contested 1972 or 1974	Lost 1972 Contested 1974
Quebec - Liberal	.05	.28
- Prog. Conservatives	.10	.18
Prairies - Liberal	.09	.19
- Prog. Conservatives	.05	.45
Ontario - Liberal	.12	.24
- Prog. Conservatives	.14	.27

distinguished Anglo-Quebeckers. Similarly, on the Prairiers the Liberals did elect a number of strong spokesmen in 1968. Most were defeated in 1972 and did not try again in 1974. In some cases, the fault may be the party's. Canadian parties may not care to encourage people to seek political careers (see Smith, 1977) or may be unable to do so given the power of local nominating conventions. In some cases, candidates of even higher quality may have contested and won the subsequent nomination — only to lose in their turn and be replaced by yet another candidate. This could be what is going on, but the electorate does not see it that way. If the average quality of candidates at each election improves with such turnover, it does not do so by a sufficient amount to increase a party's success in any region. A more plausible model underlying Table 5 is that parties do not, in general, promote political careerism and that the obstacles imposed by the present electoral system make it unlikely that regionally prestigious people will contest elections more than once for a regionally weak party. They have better things to do than to undergo repeated humiliation. Whatever the explanation, the effect of the tendencies illustrated in Table 5 are detrimental. Though the tendency is common to strong and weak regions alike, the effects are most unfortunate for a party in its weakest region. If the Liberals can elect few people on the Prairies, and if the large number who fail to be elected do not run again, voters will hardly recognize the party as the same team that solicited their support once before. Worse, they *will* recognize the party as the same outsiders they rejected before. Our parties have been fortunate in finding at least some candidates with local roots, popularity and prestige, to run at each election. Usually these are discovered only in time *for* the election. They are not available to the party — as representatives, antennae, or organization builders — between elections. If they are not political careerists, they have no incentive to be bridges between the party and local elites or local interest groups. They also have no institutionalized way of doing so. A party without a continuing commitment from people in and out of parliament is dependent on others for information relevant to policy-making and electioneering. These "others" are likely to be professionals — journalists, pollsters, media advisers, policy "experts" — but this is not political professionalism. Their advice will be more sensitive to professional norms and interests than to partisan norms and interests. Again, the party is robbed of its character and of its instrumental usefulness to the electorate.

While the growing influence of professional advertising men in politics is not now likely to be reversed, the electoral system can be a powerful instrument for the encouragement of political careers. Proportional representation systems, other than that involving the single transferable vote, require the use of lists in multi-member constituencies. For major party candidates, the top third of the list will be virtually assured election, and these positions could be used to maintain a stable party leadership and to attract spokesmen from major groups in all regions. A recent comparison of political leadership in Britain and Germany finds that former officials of interest groups are much more likely to sit as party representatives in parliament in Germany than in Britain, where interest groups by-pass the electoral arena to act directly with the bureaucracy. This difference is partly attributable to differences in the electoral system (Guttsman, 1974). A common charge (Hermens, 1941, pp. 58-66 is one example) is that systems of proportionality lead to stagnation of the political elite as the established leadership protects its own position at the top of lists and frustrates political newcomers by keeping them in unfavourable list positions. Certainly this could occur, but does not seem inherent in the system. Much depends on the commitment of list makers to the institutional interests of the party. The same British/German comparison referred to earlier found that German parliamentarians had considerably shorter careers than their British counterparts. The turnover is apparently related to greater difficulty of securing constituency nomination rather than wholesale revamping of lists (Guttsman, 1974).

The third criterion of strength may appear to contradict the first, which asserted that parties should not try to represent everybody. Are we not here saying that the party should be sensitive to everybody? Both qualities are important and there is no contradiction. Sensitivity and representation are quite distinct. Politics is mainly about interests and hence involves conflict. That is why it is dishonest, except under special conditions, to pretend that everyone can be represented. However, politics is also, in part, about meanings or symbols. Here it is possible to needlessly offend groups and complicate problems of national unity. A good example would be the very destructive air-traffic control dispute of 1976. At the overt level, the meaning seems very straight-forward: there was a question of the safety of bilingual traffic control which was eminently a debatable matter since there was no good evidence about how bilingual control under instrument rules would work in a Canadian setting (though it apparently was safe enough in other countries). However, two other sets of meanings were quickly attached to the dispute, and, while it was possible to find out on an intellectual plane what these were, parties could easily fail to appreciate them. A party with few French Canadians in its caucus could not hope to *feel* what it means to fight to have one's language used in areas of commerce and high technology and to have a door slammed in one's face on the basis of no conclusive evidence. Evidence might show a necessary conflict between safety and bilingualism. This conflict of interest not being established, the dispute became one of a conflict of status. What is more, it was a question of status within Quebec and not within Canada as a whole. The leadership and caucus of the Progressive Conservative and New Democratic parties might have obtained an intellectual appreciation of this by reading *Le Devoir* but they could not have felt the passion of it without a strong caucus from or organization in Quebec which could argue passionately.

The second set of meanings was that attached to the other side of the conflict of status. Talk shows and letters to the editor during the period of the conflict again gave good evidence of basic anti-French hostility. We can, perhaps with a claim to generosity, take at face value the position of those politicians, and others, who said that *they* were not anti-French but were backing the controllers on the question of safety. However, this argument must be seen as simultaneously a confession of insensitivity to the nature of the groups finding encouragement from these stands. The plea "I didn't know the gun was loaded" may be defensible, but the results are no less tragic.

Other, less dramatic, examples of insensitivity could easily be multiplied. Prime Minister Trudeau has managed to appear particularly unconcerned about things that affect life in the west, things ranging from wheat sales to strikes and lock-outs of brewery workers. The problem is not solely one of personality. Insensitivity could be much reduced by a large contingent of colleagues who do reflect the views and feelings of the various parts of the country and who would make it their business to communicate these to the rest of the party, and, in particular, to the party leadership. None of these insensitivities arise out of the choice of governing strategy and the trade-offs that such a strategy requires. So far, no governing strategy in Canada has precluded a party from getting votes in all provinces. Current insensitivity is needless.

The final component of strength was party direction. A party that is to have impact on government must have not only a policy character, but good information about the environment in which it governs. Only this permits them to come up with what Rose calls "not unworkable" means to achieve desired ends (Rose, 1976, chaps. 15 and 16). A party uninformed about its environment is as vulnerable as a party devoid of feedback from supporters in some region of the country. A party without governing experience is prone to administrative *gaffes* just as a party without regional or cultural antennae may fall afoul of its own insensitivity. In either case, such a party may find itself committed to policy that is unworkable, self-defeating or unexpectedly unpopular.

With respect to many of these, it is probable that the electoral system has only a relatively minor role. We have already reviewed some of the evidence. The question of party representation is probably bound up with party sensitivity. It is not the case, in Canada, that conflicts of interest between English and French Canadians are so intense that parties cannot get votes from both camps. The fact that the votes are not translated into seats, however, makes it inevitable that all parties will be needlessly insensitive to certain currents of feeling — needless, literally, because the views *could* have been present within the party but for the operation of the electoral system.

We have also noted the premium which a plurality electoral system places on appealing to the most volatile voters, by exaggerating the impact of their movement. This may induce parties to neglect the voices of traditional supporters, and this, of course, increases the incentive to every voter to be volatile in bestowing his favours. Indeed, evidence suggests that the vote is much more volatile in countries with plurality electoral systems (Rose and Urwin, 1970). The arguments about responsiveness to voters made a few pages ago rest on a view of the voter as an individual. If we shift our conception to that of the voter as a partisan, then his interest and the party interest are the same. Neither is well-served by an electoral system that over-values the behaviour of the least partisan citizens. As we have seen, virtually all electoral systems except the plurality one reward the development of a disciplined vote, even where it is not sufficiently large to elect a member by itself. In addition, proportional systems make it easier to elect members on a smaller, or less concentrated, vote.

With encouragement of representitiveness, the building of faithful voting blocs and the opportunity for developing political careers, we may suppose that proportional representation systems contribute both to the morale and to the indispensability of the party organization. Electoral systems are not uniquely powerful causal agents; it is often difficult to disentangle their effects from that of the broader political

37

histories of each country. While it is true, for example, that the European countries with PR have very extensive party organizations, we could not expect a change in electoral reform to change overnight the propensity of the federal Liberal party to neglect organization and rely on advertising agencies (Whitaker, 1977) or to immediately overcome the constant internal rivalries of the Progressive Conservative party (Perlin, forthcoming). Over the long term, a Canadian electoral system involving provincial lists might well encourage both more extensive organization and greater internal democracy. The local lawyers and businessmen who now can focus on a single constituency would need a province-wide framework if they were to influence the formation of the lists. Especially in a party's weak provinces, that would be the essential objective of those seeking political careers. In order to have any provincial organization at all, parties would have to offer avenues for province-wide action by partisans — particularly so as the barriers to entry of new parties would be lowered and established parties could ill afford creating dissatisfaction arising from feelings of exclusion from party decision-making.

Internal party rules will determine who precisely has the power to nominate lists. In the Canadian context, we could assume that provincial bodies would be very influential, and we might hope that these bodies might be forced to operate much more openly than they now do. In this respect, there might well be a spill-over from the left, as the NDP would have open procedures and would be able to offer a surer passport to parliament than it now can. There is no necessary reason to expect, as Hermens does, that the party leader will become a virtual dictator (Hermens, 1941, pp. 51-55). Indeed, the problem may be to ensure that the party leader has a sufficiently strong influence to make sure that members of his caucus follow the party line and that each carries a fair share of parliamentary work. The national leadership must also pay close attention to whose political careers are to be developed in each province. The leader does have one powerful tool since current election legislation requires him to certify the candidates of his party (Courtney, 1978, pp. 51-53).

It is beyond the scope of this work to discuss internal party rules. One possibility, however, would be to reserve the top two or three spots on any list to the total discretion of the leader (who might receive advice from a provincial convention), but then to say that the leader could not change other rankings determined by provincial conventions by more than one or two levels.

Another less attractive possibility would be to institute province-wide party primaries with positions on the lists being determined by rank-order in a province-wide vote. At first sight this might seem a useful device to stimulate party membership, but great care would have to be taken to avoid a "packing" of the primary. Candidates with lots of resources could sell memberships to large numbers of people with no continuing commitment to the party. Even if this were avoided by requiring that primary voters be members for at least twelve months and that membership dues be collected quarterly, the primary system would still be disadvantageous to the party. The primary system leads directly to intra-party factionalism. Primary campaigns might engender bitterness, and make balanced lists more difficult to achieve. A party which does harbour contending interests would try to place each group near the top of the list to make sure that all will work for the party in the general election. In a primary contest one faction might win all the top spots. The primary system could also be detrimental to career-building and might well saddle the party leader with uncongenial colleagues.

Not all proportional systems strengthen party organization. Election by single transferable vote works in much the same way as the primary system would. STV forces candidates of a single party to compete against each other as well as against their partisan opponents. In five-man constituences with a party balance of 2:2:1, incumbents are motivated to seek relatively weak running mates or to nominate less than a full slate of candidates. (For a fascinating case study, see Carty, forthcoming.) Local candidates try to build personal, not party, followings and to distinguish themselves from co-partisans. This might be benign, even laudable, where one of the candidates distinguishes himself by exceptional constituency service. It is much less attractive when one of the candidates seeks to outbid others, including his party leader, in espousing local prejudices.

This anti-party tendency is held to be a virtue by some commentators on PR/STV. This system allows voters to define their own "party". If such a system were used in Canada, we might assume that in a five-member constituency in the Eastern Townships of Quebec, for example, each party would include two English-speakers on its ticket. English-speaking voters might then shun any party list, and simply distribute their preferences over all the English-speaking candidates, thus creating a *de facto* English Canadian party in that district. Moreover, depending on the size of the voting bloc and the degree of heterogeneity of the majority, such a "party", by skillful deployment of its vote, might win more seats than the proportion of the group in the constituency. The strategy would be equally available in Saskatchewan or Alberta to French Canadians who are now underrepresented.

This anti-party tendency is undesirable. For reasons outlined at the beginning of this section, parties need organizational resources which cannot come to parties created *ad hoc* on election day. All that can be said of STV is that it might in the long run stimulate the parties to develop strong organizations as a reaction to its disaggregative effect, and as an attempt to maximize party advantage. Australia does have a strong party system, and in this setting there is very little cross-party voting or slippage between candidates of the same party in Australian Senate elections (Aitken and Kahan, 1974, p. 440). Given the present weakness of the Canadian party system, initial results under PR/STV would probably be closer to the Irish pattern. Even in Ireland, independents and party rebels are no longer as successful as they used to be, but incumbents still have no incentive to strengthen the party, as opposed to their personal, organization (Carty, 1976). The general proposition holds then: PR/STV weakens party organizations, a feature that would be particularly undesirable in the Canadian context.

Relevant to the question of organizational strength is the low barrier to entry of new parties which we have seen to be, at least formally, more likely under PR than plurality electoral systems. One could argue that this tendency is likely, by encouraging coalition cabinets, to disperse governmental experience and access to information more widely among parties, and so contribute to our fourth dimension of organizational strength. Single party monopoly of government for long periods of time would end. Parties that were occasionally represented in cabinets would develop expertise useful during their periods in opposition.

Opponents of proportional representation would impute a high cost in organizational integrity to these benefits of access. They argue that PR systems weaken parties by vastly reducing the cost of dissidence. The two effects are opposite sides of the same coin. An electoral system which gives each political formation parliamentary representation in exact ratio to its voting strength means that groups which had formerly cooperated might split apart and that politicians who had formerly worked together need no longer do so. In appraising this argument we must try to distinguish between those party splits which would be socially consequential, and those which would not.

Consider the present state of the major Canadian parties. The Progressive Conservative party must broker at least the interests of Western Canada and industrial Ontario — possibly of Quebec as well — if it is to form a government. The Liberals must bridge the interests of Quebec and industrial Ontario. Both gain support in the Atlantic region. The opponents of PR argue that the present plurality system gives parties an important whip to crack to keep spokesmen for these various interests in line. Any party split would probably lead to the electoral defeat of both the original party and the new fragment. Such an argument is particularly persuasive if support for the different wings of the party is not territorially concentrated. Britain's plurality electoral system is at least a partial explanation of the ability of the British Labour party to keep its socialist and social democratic wings in harness. The argument has less weight when the differing interests − economic or cultural − are also geographically defined. The plurality system does not bar, and may even overrepresent, a revived French Canadian nationalist party of the *Bloc Populaire* type. The same would hold for a Prairie party. The data in Table 4 suggests that there exists opportunities for new parties. A cost of forcing social groups with real competing interests to fuzz over these in an attempt at cooperation is that the brokerage parties generate relatively little affect or commitment from the electorate.

Why, then, have regionalist parties not arisen in the postwar period? The question implies what needs to be demonstrated: that the existing parties are not regionalist. We have already noted that both the Liberal and the Progressive Conservative parties are less national, in the make-up of their caucuses, than they have been in the past. However, they are not the *Bloc Populaire* or the Party of Western Canada. That such parties do not exist to any significant extent probably reflects barriers to entry arising elsewhere than in the electoral system. The interests to which they might appeal may find it more promising to work through provincial governments, and the elite population which might provide the activists for new parties may not be sufficiently large to sustain activity at both the federal and the provincial levels. Various rules for allocating broadcast time, public subsidies, and the right to issue receipts for political donations favour established over new parties. It is also true that the present electoral system has the virtue of creating uncertainty. A new regionalist party might sweep to an overwhelming victory or might suffer a humiliating defeat − either possibility being consistent with a given level of voter support, once parties get around 25% of the vote. Moreover, under the current electoral system a single regionalist party will inevitably find itself in opposition. Only if several regionalist parties arose simultaneously could the present duopoly on government be broken. However, given regionally concentrated interests, the plurality electoral system offers only weak support to an established party system. Whether or not there will be fragmentation is probably more dependent on the degree of alienation of a social group from the national party system and on its interest in working through the institutions of that system. Over the long run, such a group will evolve a leadership to launch a new alternative and a degree of voter commitment needed to cross the initial hurdles. This is, in schematic form, the history of the *Parti Québécois*. Quite despite the barriers of the electoral system, interests present but not dominant in the then current provincial parties left them to form a new one and were able to sustain that new party through eight years of parliamentary underrepresentation. The same marshalling of political resources would be needed for a new political party to arise under proportional representation. The major contribution of PR would be to reduce the uncertainty somewhat. New parties would have greater assurance of parliamentary representation right from the beginning and this would make it easier for them to recruit and support a leadership since the parliamentarians would be paid from the public purse. However, the new party would still be uncertain of gaining the attention of the government.

Would the rise of new parties be detrimental? We shall return to this in the next section on policy-making. We may note in passing that such new parties would be likely to reduce the alienation of voters from the parliamentary system. Voters finding a party unequivocally committed to their interests would, one presumes, have a greater sense that party politics mattered than do voters under the present party system. The apparent harmony within the present parties is only apparent. The social reality is that the groups within the Liberal and Progressive Conservative parties do have competing interests and that neither party has articulated a programme which creatively redefines the interests of each group to overcome the competition.

Under PR, new parties could arise which would be less socially significant. Besides conflicting social interests there also exist conflicting personal interests, ambitions and rivalries. These, too, one might argue, are subordinated because of the operation of our electoral system. In this case, however, there is less advantage in letting them emerge. No social interest is furthered, and no voter alienation is reduced by a party split solely on these grounds. Clearly the issue is overstated here, but we could think of a continuum of party splits ranging from high to low social significance. Is it worth avoiding splits of low significance even at the price of failing to have party splits that would definitely advantage some parts of the society? Is this a necessary trade-off? The second question is easier to answer than the first. It is unlikely that any proportional electoral system really encourages party splits where these are largely devoid of social significance. The recent emergence of the Australian Democrats, a dissident wing of the Liberal Party and led by a former Minister dropped from the cabinet, may be a case in point. A proportional system allows dissidents to try to build up a following for a new party with which to bargain in furtherance of their ambitions. This no doubt could occur but it is bad for the original host party only when the splitter manages to achieve some decisive electoral or parliamentary position. Otherwise, the splitter has very little to bargain with, as is presently the case in Australia, and will either have to accept the ending of a political career or a somewhat ignominious reintegration with his original party. Probably the closest Canadian parallel to Don Chipp, the leader of the Australian Democrats, is Paul Hellyer. It is possible that, with a different

42

electoral system, his Action Canada party would have had seats in parliament, but it is not certain that his position would have been any better. It would only if he could have captured a substantial portion of discontent with the Liberal party. If this discontent were regionally based, he could accomplish the same ends under the present electoral system.

A change to a proportional electoral system with lists in Canada would, at least in the short term, strengthen the existing political parties and the party system more generally. It would allow parties to develop political careers for spokesmen in all regions and, as a consequence, to be more sensitive to needs in all regions. Parties would be encouraged to extend their organization as far as possible, and this might stabilize their voting base. Parties moving in and out of government coalitions would benefit from the experience in power. One can confidently predict for the short term because it takes time to marshall the resources needed before a new party could emerge. In the long run, existing parties could be badly weakened by the emergence of new, more socially homogeneous parties. With PR and the rise of a new party, the Quebec Conservative party could be reduced to the third of its Quebec voters who are now committed supporters. Ironically, the Conservatives would still get more seats in Quebec than at present. The fate of the Liberal party on the Prairies could be similar. Each might be weaker in those regions in the longer term than they would have been immediately after PR. It is highly unlikely that either party would be eliminated from any region or that its caucus would be more regionally imbalanced than it is at present. Presumably the emergence of new parties would be a further stimulus to organizational elaboration of the established parties. However, if new parties did emerge with some strength after two or three elections, the major present parties would be smaller than they are now. Minority or coalition governments would become the norm. It is this prospect that we evaluate in the next section.

D. Policy-making Capacity

"Fair Representation" has always been the banner under which proponents of PR have fought. "Effective Government" is the counter slogan of the opposing forces. In the review to this point we have found that PR electoral systems do mirror more faithfully the first preferences (among parties) of the electorate, and that STV and Alternative Voting give a better reflection of preferences among candidates. The present electoral system distorts representation of parties and candidates. We have also speculated that PR, in some form using party lists, would strengthen parties as organizations, improve the morale of party organizations, add to the sensitivity of the party caucus, and encourage parties to establish closer links with their electorate. Are these gains costless?

There is now a considerable literature arguing that governments in industrial or post-industrial societies are "overloaded". The argument is that in such societies there are many different groups defined along a bewildering variety of dimensions: economic sectors, sexual and life style preferences, life cycle positions, cultural attachments, and so on. All are competing for political attention. A government attempting to acknowledge all of them would be paralyzed by an inability to focus its attention on any problem. Government can only profitably deal with a few issues at a time, and needs "gate-keepers" to reduce the proliferation of demands on its attention. The plurality electoral system is seen as such a gate-keeper. If all these demands were represented in the parliament, all would have some means to compel government attention and collectively to engender government paralysis.

Proportional representation systems, runs the argument, do not act as such a gate-keeper. Rather, they change the party system along two dimensions in the long run:

1. they multiply the number of parties;
2. they increase the ideological dispersion of the party system.

The first part of the claim is much easier to test empirically. PR systems do tend, on average, to have more parties than plurality systems. The alleged tendency of the latter to resolve party conflict to two contestants is less well-established, with Canada standing as a glaring exception.

As a result of the multiplicity of parties, and their representation in reasonably close proportion to their popular vote, single party majority government becomes unlikely. While minority governments occur under plurality electoral systems, the number of parties with which they must form overt or tacit alliances is small under such systems. Of the seven minority Parliaments in Canada since 1921, governments have been able to survive with the support of one other party. Since 1957, governments could only have been defeated by a combination of three parties. In democracies with proportional representation systems, governments tend to be formal coalitions rather than tacit understandings and they spread over more political parties. Between 1946 and 1965 in Canada, all governments were single-party. Over the same period for eleven European countries with some form of PR, governments had an average of 2.3 parties. The high was for the Netherlands with seventeen years of four-party government and three years of two-party government. The governments of Norway and Sweden were almost as *monocolore* as Canada's. The first had nineteen years of single-party government, and the latter fourteen years despite having quite strict PR

44

systems. (Calculated from data presented in the appendix to Blondel, 1968).

Whether this means that bargaining costs are higher within governments of PR rather than plurality systems is a question we shall put off for the moment. Certainly the overt bargaining costs will be higher, and the fact that parties have separate identities may make it more difficult for agreement to be achieved or to endure. (On the increasing length of time needed to form governments in the Netherlands, see Daalder, forthcoming). Measuring the duration of governments in days, Taylor and Herman (1971, pp. 30-31) do find this to be negatively correlated with the fractionalization of the parliament and with the fractionalization of its own support. Neither coefficient (-.448 and -.307) is particularly high.

The argument that PR encourages ideological dispersion of the party system is developed as follows. Under any political system, parties compete with those other parties most similar to themselves. In plurality systems, all parties compete for the median voter. Under PR, parties compete for the same bloc of voters with other parties whose position is closest to their own. There is no necessary tendency to compete for the median voter; rather, the competition is with those parties to one's immediate "right" and to one's immediate "left". Social democrats compete against liberals and against socialists for a moderately reformist bloc. Socialists also compete against Communists, liberals against centrists. The need to fight a "two-front" war complicates the maintenance of internal unity for each party. It is said to have two other effects as well:

1. parties attempt to outbid each other and hence promise social benefits beyond what the economy could tolerate;
2. parties are reluctant to co-operate with each other in government since this would blur the distinctiveness that each seeks in an effort to improve its competitive position.

A more plausible example in Canada might be that, if a change of electoral system encouraged the formation of a distinctively French Canadian party, and if such a party entered a coalition with English Canadian parties, it would soon find its flanks threatened by an even more extremist French Canadian party. This party would make demands which the English Canadian parties could not accept. Because of its stance it would win the most votes in Quebec but would go into an isolated opposition, and national institutions would be further discredited in the eyes of the *Québécois*.

A slight variant of this scenario holds that, in times of economic difficulty, when restriction of demand and, in particular, of government spending seem indicated, a PR system encourages parties to shun their responsibilities. To gain a competitive advantage in subsequent elections, coalition partners would be tempted to pull out of a coalition, and leave to others the odium of being associated with unpopular measures.

One suspects that parliamentarism itself contains strong centripetal incentives. To put the matter in extreme terms, imagine a game in which players were regions and in which a majority subset of players had to form, which, when formed, had the power to exploit those areas left out (Riker, 1962; Browne, 1971). In this game, we could assume that few would put a high price on joining the coalition. Coalition instability is likely as losers attempt to entice some member away from the coalition. The parliamentary game would respond to similar incentives. Groups would seek to join governmental coalitions in order to protect their own positions. Only groups with no prospect of ever being part of a government would tend towards extremism. The growth of "Eurocommunism" seems to indicate that the prospect of inclusion in government is a sufficient condition for moderation and that actual inclusion in government is unnecessary. This is not to deny that some groups might contest parliamentary elections with no intention of taking part in government but with the sole objective of discrediting the whole system. Such "anti-system" parties were present in the classic cases of political instability: Weimar Germany, IVth Republic France, and Italy in the two immediate postwar periods. They could arise in Canada. However, whether or not they do depends much more on the political and social history of a state than on its electoral system. Moreover, as we have repeatedly stressed, should the population of Quebec or the Prairies become so alienated as to sustain an anti-system party, there is little reason to expect the present electoral system to block its rise.

The scenarios of ideological dispersion have considerable formal plausibility and can be derived from a model of the electorate distributed in such a way that there are many nodes of voters in the policy space (Downs, 1957). That such a scenario inevitably leads to political extremism and collapse of government is much more problematic. Logically such a model requires an electorate which does not have fixed policy preferences but which responds to cues from party leaders. It also requires that such cues always be centrifugal. Neither assumption necessarily holds. The parliamentary "game", as we have just seen, may encourage moderation. In many multi-party systems, certain parties are so central in the ideological space that they are guaranteed membership in government whatever the election outcome. These parties will certainly respond more to governing incentives than to electoral incentives. They will be careful not to take positions which would complicate their assimilation into a new government. Even more ideologically extreme parties will not necessarily be driven to an anti-system stance solely for electoral reasons. Indeed, the major Communist parties in Europe now

46

have quite secure electoral bases and are relatively free to respond to governing rather than to electoral calculations. This may be the major difference between the postwar and interwar periods. Much of the theory and evidence on which PR systems are condemned come from the interwar periods for countries where the legal existence of certain parties was a quite recent phenomenon and where populations were severely alienated as a result of war and economic collapse. In the post Second World War period many parties began with heightened legitimacy as a result of their roles in the resistence. Though the countries had been devastated, postwar reconstruction and an economic boom meant that populations were not so alienated and volatile. However that may be, ideological dispersion in parliaments or governments does not seem related to governmental stability. The Taylor and Herman study already cited found that the correlations of stability with ideological fragmentation was a bit weaker than the correlation of stability with fragmentation measured solely in terms of the numbers and strengths of the parties in a parliament (Taylor and Herman, 1971, p. 34).

The argument linking irrationalities, delays, and inconsistencies in policy-making to the incentives supplied by the magnification of electoral considerations by particular systems of representation has, more recently, been turned against the plurality system. These are the ones now seen as most likely to encourage a shunning of responsibility or a desperate search to distinguish oneself from one's competitor or predecessor in government (Finer, 1975, pp. 26-29). Professor Wilson (1975) buttresses the last charge with his analysis of British policies for regional development since 1945. Under successive governments policy has undergone a series of changes which, though far from fundamental, are enough to affect the calculations of those firms which might be induced to locate in areas to be favoured. Both the idea that a new government might create less favourable incentives, or that new government might create more favourable incentives, lead businessmen to avoid making any commitment at all, and so defeats the broader objective of the policy.

Similarly, some British scholars, partisans of reform towards a more proportional system in that country, argue that a system of proportional representation is more favourable than a plurality system for incremental policy-making or "fine-tuning" of the economy. Again, the argument is that the plurality system forces an adversary relationship between the ins and the outs, such that changes of government tend to bring about large changes in the policy pursued by the predecessor even when the successor has less than a majority of the popular vote. The nationalization-denationalization-renationalization of the British steel industry or the imposition-abandonment-reimposition of an incomes policy in Britain is evidence of such non-incremental policy-making (Stout, 1975).

What is less clear is the role of the electoral system in all of this. Commentators anticipate that, with a change in electoral systems, British governments would either be longer lived or would, at least, have more cabinet continuity than is now the case (Finer, 1975, p. 23). It is true that in the Scandinavian countries, Germany or Australia there has been little turnover of government since the war. However, when turnover did occur, it led to a large change in personnel with little or no overlap between the successor and predecessor governments. Continuity is therefore to be explained by the stability of the preferences of the electorate rather than by the effects of the electoral system. The British scholars may be entertaining a Dutch scenario whereby the electorate is more volatile but one party is always so strategically placed in parliament as to be included in every government. Here, continuity of at least some government personnel may more easily be attributed to the electoral system and may explain some portion of the continuity of policy. In general, however, if the desideratum is marginal policy change over several elections, it seems more plausible to see this resulting from basic consensus and from more elaborate alternative mechanisms for the consultation of affected interests. A PR system in Canada would probably end single-party monopoly of office, although this is not guaranteed. Conceivably a single party could choose to hold office as a minority government. Once the system were established, elections would no longer produce either zero change or total change in the partisan composition of the government.

Much more comparative research would be needed to determine the effect of the stability of personnel on the rationality and continuity of policy. It may be that, with less change likely to result from any election, policy will be framed with more long-run considerations in view. In looking for evidence of a partisan-inspired economic cycle (indicated by more growth in real disposable income in election than in non-election years), Tufte finds eight countries where such a cycle is *not* in evidence (Tufte, 1978, p. 12). All have PR systems and include Austria, Denmark, the Federal Republic of Germany, Italy and the Netherlands. A PR electoral system may be a necessary condition for avoiding the temptations of political manipulation of the economy, but it is clearly not sufficient and one would want to examine many more dimensions before concluding that policy-making was superior under one form of electoral system than under some other form. The ideology of the major governing party seems at least as important in accounting for "appropriate" responsiveness to macroeconomic conditions (Cowart, 1978a, 1978b).

To sum up the argument of this sub-section so far, the adoption of proportional representation in Canada would increase the number of parties needed to sustain a government and create a pattern of institutional interests which might reduce the longevity of cabinets. On the other hand, there is no reason to believe that cabinet-making and policy-making would become impossible. In formal terms, policy-making and cabinet-formation by a single brokerage party is usually described as a purely cooperative game. Where several parties are involved in a more overt process of bargaining, the game becomes a mixed one with cooperative and competitive elements. All members of the government benefit from successful management of those aspects of policy on which there is high consensus, but each must conciliate its own electorate on other matters and each may have designs on some portion of the electorate of its partners. The latter effect allegedly does not complicate bargaining within a brokerage party, although one could imagine situations making that a mixed game as well. Although Prairie Liberals do not try to "raid" the electorate of Ontario Liberals, they do disagree on strategy. Is the next election best fought by strengthening one's appeal to Ontario or to the Prairies? Institutional interests come into play here as well, though perhaps in a more circumscribed fashion since scission of a party is much more costly to all elements than is the rupture of a government. The weight of institutional interest does facilitate the concluding of bargains within the brokerage party but these may be at the expense of the weaker partner and at a cost of increasing regional alienation.

It is difficult to be more precise about the effects of the introduction of some form of PR on policy-making in Canada since one cannot predict exactly what kind of a party system would arise. Canada would continue to have two national brokerage parties. Each party caucus would be more heterogeneous than it is at present: both would have less weight in parliament than they do now when they are in government. If no new parties emerge, one could predict that policy-bargaining would be more two-dimensional than at present. In addition to cleavages organized around culture and region, class cleavages would be more prominently represented in parliament, as the NDP would be strengthened and would be a potent force in government formation. If specific regionalist parties did emerge, regional interests would find that they had more political options than they now have. Quebec interests could continue to back the Liberals, or to back a Quebec party which might enter governments with the Progressive Conservative party. Prairie interests could continue to back the PCs or to support parties that would be negotiating with other political forces. In either the "new-party" or the "no-new-party" outcome, there would be many more potential governing combinations. While this might mean delay in settling on any of them and would enhance the vulnerability of that one to subsequent enticement of one of its members by other groups, the new parliaments would allow much more innovative response, at least initially, than seems possible under the present system.

E. Selecting Campaign Tactics

Campaign strategy and tactics are difficult to disentangle from governing strategy and tactics. Many of the topics included under earlier headings could also be included under this one, and we shall only briefly review the previous argument:

1. to the extent that elections under PR are less affected by marginal or volatile voters, governing parties have less incentive to manipulate policy for short run ends. Macroeconomic manipulation should be less subject to electoral calculation;
2. to the extent that parties are more representative and sensitive, and that leaders can effectively discipline followers, campaigns should be less marked by cultural slurs;
3. to the extent that extreme groups already find parliamentary representation, established governing parties will be less likely to flirt with such opinion.

One question of tactics has not so far been considered. Is the personalization of electoral campaigns more likely under plurality than under proportional electoral sysems? The argument that it is runs as follows: electoral systems which produce single-party majorities make it more likely that government itself is personalized. The Prime Minister gains the bulk of media attention, and will, if so inclined, dominate his party's campaign as well. Whether he does or not, elections will turn on his qualities which can much more easily be grasped by voters than can questions of policy. Trudeaumania was but a more swinging version of "Uncle Louis". Campaigns may, of course, pivot around a personality in a negative sense, as for Dave Barrett in British Columbia or Trudeau in 1979. Whether positive or negative, the quality of voter decision-making is diminished.

By contrast, an electoral system producing coalition governments affords prominence to many party leaders, and cabinet colleagues from other parties will not accept in good grace the especial prominence of one of their colleague-competitors who happens to be the prime minister. While the argument is plausible, conclusive evidence is lacking. One suspects that the tendency to personalization is more strictly a function of demands of media technology, particularly television, than of the operation of the electoral system. Certainly the personality of the Dutch

Socialist party leader, den Uyl, was a very strong one during the course of his prime ministership and in the subsequent election campaign. German campaigns also seem highly personalized, though there one is dealing with a better approximation to a two-party system than often exists in Canada.

4 A New Electoral System for Canada

Electoral systems produce, or tend to produce, many different kinds of outcomes. Different observers would value each differently but few would be perfectly satisfied with any single system. This, in itself, might be a sufficient argument for the adoption of a mixed electoral system such as the one used in the Federal Republic of Germany. Mixed systems are characterized by having two classes of parliamentary representative: one group representing constituencies; the other representing some more inclusive unit – a province, or perhaps, the whole country. In this section, one particular mixed system will be proposed. In the next section, it will be compared with several other mixed systems mooted for Canada.

Any system which preserves territorial constituencies represented by a single parliamentarian has the advantage both of conforming more closely to Canadian traditions as well as of preserving the attractive functional features of such systems. The proposal below is designed with the following principles in mind:

1. parliamentary seats, whether constituency seats or at large seats, are allocated according to population. The constituencies are to be as equal in population as is consistent with recognizing established communities, natural boundaries and with preserving manageable size;
2. voting consists of a single choice among candidates, only one of whom represents any given party in the constituency. Ballots would contain the names of the parties they represent if they are legally recognized.

Both features are identical with current practice.

In designing any such system, one has to decide the balance between constituency level and at large seats. Part of the calculation also involves consideration of the total size of the legislature. One could, for example, take the current size of the House of Commons as fixed and simply sub-divide it between the two levels. At the other extreme, one could treat existing constituencies as sacrosanct and graft on the additional at large seats. Of the values considered in the previous sections, one is primarily at stake in this decision. Given that the following proposal treats the province as the larger unit to obtain at large seats, there must be sufficient of the latter so that each province obtains more than one such seat. The more provincial representatives there are, the better will each province's parliamentary delegation reflect the proportionate strength of the parties within the province. The fewer provincial representatives there are, the less likely the system is to offset the unrepresentativeness of the present one. The balance between constituency and provincial representatives reflects the balance of one's preference for proportional or plurality electoral systems. The present proposal involves enlarging the House of Commons by one-quarter, from 282 to 354 seats, and simultaneously reducing the number of directly represented constituencies by one-third, from 282 to 188. The ratio of constituency to provincial seats is thus 53:47. Average constituency size increases by one-half. The distribution among provinces is displayed in Table 6. Since the system is a mixed one, thresholds of exclusion are only approximate. The effective threshold of representation is one-half the number of voters in the smallest constituency in each province. The actual threshold of exclusion may be somewhat higher than that listed in Table 6. If there existed more than four parties in Newfoundland, each with more than one-tenth the vote and none winning a constituency, only the four largest would be able to find parliamentary representation. Given a commitment to representation by population, thresholds of exclusion will be unequal among provinces. These inequalities might be reduced by having a set of "Atlantic Provinces" representatives or "Prairie plus Northern" representatives, however, the reduction would perhaps be more formal than real. Depending on the interest, it might be easier to win 17% of the vote in Prince Edward Island than 2.5% of the vote in the Atlantic Provinces.

Taking the system described in Table 6, political parties desiring to elect provincial representatives would have to provide the chief electoral officer with eleven lists (one for each jurisdiction in the Table), each with a number of names equal to the number of provincial representatives and listed in rank order. On election night, votes would be tabulated in each constituency and the candidate with the highest total would be declared elected from that constituency. So far, there has been no change from current practice. However, the votes for candidates of each recognized party which had submitted provincial lists would be aggregated to the

Table 6

Current and Proposed Distribution of House of Commons Seats Among the Provinces

Prov.	Current	Proposed Mixed System			
		Constituency Seats	Provincial Seats	Total Seats	Threshold of Exclusion
NFLD	7	5	4	9	.10
P.E.I.	4	3	2	5	.17
N.B.	10	7	5	12	.08
N.S.	11	7	7	14	.07
QUE.	75	50	44	94	.013
ONT.	95	63	56	119	.011
MAN.	14	9	9	18	.05
SASK.	14	9	9	18	.05
ALTA.	21	14	12	26	.04
B.C.	28	19	16	35	.03
NORTH	3	2	2	4	.20
TOTAL	282	188	166	354	

provincial level, and the percentage distribution of the provincial vote so aggregated would be calculated. The total number of provincial seats (constituency plus provincial representatives) would be multiplied by each party's percentage of the provincial vote, yielding each party's provincial "entitlement". If the number of constituencies won exceeds the entitlement for any party, no action is taken. All constituencies are represented by their most popular candidate. Where the number of constituency victories is less than the entitlement, sufficient candidates from the party's provincial list are declared elected to make up the entitlement, beginning at the top of the list and skipping over any person already elected from a constituency. (As this implies, a candidate could offer himself both in a constituency and on the list.)

Table 7 shows how the 1974 election might have come out under the parliament and electoral system proposed for Table 6, assuming that vote shares had remained unchanged and that each party's success in winning constituencies was unchanged from 1974. Neither assumption is plausible, but the number of alternative scenarios is simply too vast to be discussed intelligibly. The simulation confirms many of the claims we have reviewed. Where the actual outcome awarded the Liberals 53% of the seats for 43% of the vote, and gave the NDP only 6% of the seats for their 15% of the vote, the proposed mixed system produces a proportional outcome. As a result, the NDP occupies a strategic parliamentary position as neither of the major parties has a majority of the seats.

In increasing its representation, the NDP wins seats in all provinces

54

Table 7

A Simulation of the 1974 Election under the System Proposed in Table 6

Prov.	MP	LIB.	PC	NDP	S.C.	IND.	TOTAL
NFLD.	const.	3	2				5
	prov.	1	2	1			4
	total	4	4	1			9
P.E.I.	const.	1	2				3
	prov.	1	1				2
	total	2	3				5
N.B.	const.	4	2			1	7
	prov.	2	2	1			5
	total	6	4	1		1	12
N.S.	const.	1	5	1			7
	prov.	5	2				7
	total	6	7	1			14
QUE.	const.	41	2		7		50
	prov.	10	18	7	9		44
	total	51	20	7	16		94
ONT.	const.	39	18	6			63
	prov.	15	24	17			56
	total	54	42	23			119
MAN.	const.	2	6	1			9
	prov.	3	3	3			9
	total	5	9	4			18
SASK.	const.	2	6	1			9
	prov.	3	1	5			9
	total	5	7	6			18
ALTA.	const.		14				14
	prov.	7	2	2	1		12
	total	7	16	2	1		26
B.C.	const.	7	11	1			19
	prov.	5	4	7			16
	total	12	15	8			35
NORTH	const.		1	1			2
	prov.	1	1				2
	total	1	2	1			4
CANADA	seats (%)	43	36	15	5	0.3	
	vote %	43	35	15	5	0.9	
	seat % (actual)	53	36	6	4	0.4	

but Prince Edward Island. The caucuses of the major parties are much more representative of the whole country. While MPs from Quebec actually made up 43% of the Liberal caucus but only3% of the PC caucus in 1974, under the proposed scheme Quebec would have 33% of the Liberal caucus, 16% of the PC caucus plus seven NDP members (13% of that party's caucus) where there were no such members before. The opposite kind of compensation occurs in the west. While the three prairie provinces contributed 38% of the PC caucus and 4% of the Liberal caucus in 1974; the proportions would have been 25% and 11% under the assumptions of the simulation. BC MPs would go from 6 to 8% of the Liberal caucus and from 14 to 12% of the PC caucus. Ontario would have had a little less weight with the Liberals and more with the Conservatives, while the reverse would have been true for the Atlantic provinces. (Since we have preserved representation by population, each province has the same parliamentary weight as it had before, only more equally distributed among the parties.) Insofar as party-building and career development is concerned, we cannot simulate the lists established by the political parties. We have no way of knowing how they would rank potential candidates. It may be noted, however, that all the parties gain at least some provincial seats in every province except for the NDP in P.E.I., Nova Scotia and the North. The Liberals get between 3 and 7 seats in each of the western provinces. The Progressive Conservatives get 18 in Quebec. The number of provincial representatives elected by a party will be, in part, a function of its success in winning constituencies. The 1974 election was probably not atypical in this respect, so the number of provincial representatives in Table 7 is a reasonable indication of the number of "safe" seats each party would have in each province in the short term. All parties would be able to guarantee careers to a significant number of politicians from all regions and thereby seek better contact with, and information from, the various regional communities making up the country.

Not all agree about the party-building virtues of a system of dual representation. Some active federal politicians, notably Mark Mac-Guigan and Walter Baker, told Jeffrey Simpson that creating "two classes of MPs" would introduce further invidious distinctions into the caucus (The Globe and Mail, March 20, 1979, p.7). This objection is difficult to evaluate. Does a difference in area represented — province as opposed to constituency — create a difference in status? If so, who is on top?

The politicians feel that, because of our traditions, the MP directly elected by local voters would have the greater claim to legitimacy. This may be an accurate rendering of voter psychology, at least in the initial stages. We have already seen, however, that the ability to capture a constituency, or the fact of having lost one, are poor guides to the merit of a candidate. Very attractive candidates lose to even more attractive candidates as in the 1978 Rosedale by-election. Winning candidates can obtain seats with relatively low popular support, as long as the opposition is split among two or more parties. The vote for each candidate is determined by attitudes to leaders, parties and issues which may override judgements on the candidates themselves. For all these reasons, constituency MPs' claims to superior ability or popularity are somewhat dubious.

So too would be their claim to have carried the provincial representatives on their backs. At least some provincial representatives will have contested constituencies unsuccessfully. They will, therefore, have contributed to the provincial totals that won the provincial seats. Could the fact that they had lost constituencies be held against them? Not if one accepts the argument of the preceeding paragraph. Provincial representatives are not without constituencies. They simply don't represent small geographical areas. The good provincial representative would hasten to develop links with interests which are important provincially but which may not be concentrated territorially. Where a constituency MP courts local professionals and chambers of commerce, the provincial MP would find it profitable to develop links with auto parts manufacturers or medical researchers or certain labour unions. Many criteria could be used to determine where a person stands on his party list. Provincial representation could be used to reward party hacks. However the more enterprising party would use it to reward those politicians able to develop province-wide support for the party.

In raising the question of relative status, commentators appear ambivalent. While suggesting that the traditional constituency representative has the greater legitimacy, they also see the provincial MP as having a privileged status. He has been virtually guaranteed election, and voters may feel that he has *greater* legitimacy, at least in the eyes of his party leadership, than the constituency MP who did not make the list at all or who was unfavourably placed on it. In this view, some constituency campaigners will have the albatross of their party's unfavourable judgement to explain to constituency workers and local voters. There is merit in this fear, but such distinctions are made all the time. Among those already in parliament, there are front-benchers and back-benchers. Among those running for the first time, it is usually pretty clear which are the "stars" and which are not; which get the most campaign support from the party leadership and which do not. While the presence of a list makes these differences more explicit, it may also ensure that top list positions are reserved for people who really can mobilize province-wide support. The proposed system, with voters casting but a single vote, was quite deliberately designed to make party success dependent on the ability to run strong local campaigns. Managing morale among local activists is never an easy task. It becomes an even more important quality for party leadership under the present system. Reserving the top list positions either for party hacks or for technocrats unwilling to build political bases would undermine morale most certainly. Giving top posts to those who do work hard to develop contacts with province-wide groups should enhance party morale.

Parties may have to develop other compensations for those not highly placed on lists. They may develop known career rules by which better positioning could be earned. There is certainly no reason to make cabinet posts the exclusive preserve of provincial representatives. Even apart from considerations of morale, other factors would ensure that the majority of cabinet ministers represented local constituencies. In most provinces, a party's most talented candidates do win constituencies, often by large margins. If they had been placed high on the list, they would be skipped over and the provincial seats would be allocated to middle ranked candidates. In these cases, a party's strongest candidates would have helped to elect more junior ones. They could not expect immediate preferment but would have to serve their apprenticeship and establish their claim for recognition.

High position *on* a list, under this proposal, does not necessitate that a representative be elected *from* the list. Those who win constituencies remain constituency representatives. Except in provinces where the electoral system is badly biassed against a party, lists serve mainly to identify and test new candidates. This will be the situation in most provinces. Where parties are severely penalized by the electoral system, their leading lights and their provincial MPs will be the same, but this will be a minority in each party. The dual representation system does mean that no one gets into a cabinet or shadow cabinet simply by being a sole survivor of the constituency wars in some province. It also does not mean that party front benchers are insulated from direct contact with voters.

Provincial MPs could turn out to be a privileged caste, but this should not be the case. High list position could complicate party morale unless it is reserved for people who are able to enhance party support on a province-wide basis. Even so, high list position would not create cabinets composed only of provincial representatives. Similarly, the constituency MPs might claim greater legitimacy than their provincial counterparts, but should not. Ability to win a constituency is not an infallible test of merit or popularity.

5 Other Proposed Electoral System Reforms

Before introducing and commenting on other electoral system reforms proposed for Canada, it is perhaps worth noting the three main departures of the preceding proposal from the West German electoral system. In the Federal Republic of Germany, each voter casts two votes, one for a constituency candidate, and one for the *Land* (provincial) list. This gives the voter the option to support an attractive candidate without supporting his party — an option not available under our proposed system. The proposal is less of a change from the present method of voting than the West German system would be, but the justification goes beyond preserving a familiar system. Where voters cast only a single ballot, parties will have an incentive to nominate strong candidates and mount vigorous campaigns in each constituency. With a two-ballot system in Canada, one might expect parties naming token local candidates and putting a disproportionate amount of campaign resources in province-wide media campaigns. Even the Canadian provinces are not homogeneous. If the object is to reduce alienation by motivating parties to develop roots throughout provinces, a single ballot system seems indicated. The voter is not robbed of any option: he now may face the choice between party and candidate. Moreover, given findings on voter knowledge about candidates, voter use of party labels, and the advantage of incumbency effects, it is unlikely that many voters now are able to make a reasoned choice among candidates considered apart from their party.

Secondly, the second votes cast in Germany are totalled within the *Lander* but allocated nationally. *Land* totals for each party are divided by a series of successive integers (the d'Hondt system), and seats are allocated according to highest quotients — that is, the first SPD *land* seat will be allocated to that SPD *Land* list with the highest quotient; the second to the

59

Land list with the second highest quotient, and so on. (For a fuller description see Roberts, 1975). The net result is that the largest *Lander* (or the ones with the highest turnout) are somewhat over-represented in the *Bundestag*. Given the strength of provincial feeling in Canada, fixed seat allocations seem preferable.

Finally, in the Federal Republic of Germany, parties must show a certain minimum of strength before being entitled to participate in the allocation of *Land* seats. Currently, a party must win three constituencies directly or must obtain 5% of the national list votes. Under the scheme proposed in the previous section, allocations take place at the provincial level. To insist upon a 5% *national* cutoff before any movement can get provincial representative seats would discredit the system among many provincial political forces: the *Parti Acadien*, for example, or a *Bloc Populaire*-style nationalist but federalist party in Quebec, or the equivalent in the West. To legislate a 5% *provincial* cutoff would be redundant for six of the provinces anyway, since their thresholds of exclusion are already at that level or higher. Even in the other four provinces, a party with 4% of the vote, for example, would win no more than 4 seats in Quebec, 5 in Ontario, or 1 each in Alberta and British Columbia. The role of such minor parties in a 354 seat house would be negligible; so would their potential for disruption of the system, assuming that the cutoff is aimed at excluding extremist groups. Provincial cutoff margins would therefore have little practical effect. Minimum seat victories would have even less: parties winning a disproprotionately high number of constituencies in any province will get no provincial seats in any event. Given that the proposed system would work this way, one might as well leave it as formally open as possible.

A. The Smiley Proposal

Early in 1978, Professor Donald Smiley of York University offered a proposal also involving a distinction between constituency and provincial representatives. He described its workings as follows:

> "Voters would cast their ballots as they now do and the same number of MP's would be elected from single member districts. But the House of Commons would be enlarged to include 100 'provincial' MP's, with PEI having one of these and the rest distributed among the other provinces in proportion to their respective populations. . . . the provincial MP's would be chosen by ranking in each province those candidates who had received the highest proportion of popular votes to the winning candidates. Thus in Newfoundland which according to the

60

1971 census would gain two seats under my proposal the provincial members would be those who had come nearest to capturing the seven seats in the province." (Smiley, 1978, p. 85).

In the Smiley proposal, the ratio of constituency to provincial representatives is nearly 3:1, which makes it difficult to compare with the proposal in the previous section. It is clear from the structure of the Smiley system that the top two parties in any province are especially favoured. This effect is probably exaggerated as the proportion of provincial representatives declines. As a result of this bias, the NDP gains no additional seats in any province where it fails to win seats under strict plurality rule. In other words, the system is still biassed against third parties attempting national appeals, and relatively favourable to regional third parties. Professor Smiley, simulating the 1972 and 1974 results under his reform, showed that Social Credit was able to increase its seats by more than 50% in both 1972 and 1974 over the number of constituencies won, while the NDP increased its seats by 33% in 1972 and 40% in 1974. The Smiley reform is also less favourable to the Progressive Conservatives in Quebec and to the Liberals in the West than is the system here proposed, as we shall see in a moment. Moreover, the actual outcome under the Smiley proposal is highly dependent on where the votes are. In 1972, with 17% of the Quebec vote, the Progressive Conservatives gain only three of that province's 28 provincial seats (11%) and only five of 102 seats (5%) in total. In 1974, with 21% of the Quebec vote, the PC's get 11 of 28 provincial seats (39%) and 14 of 102 seats (14%). The effect is probably less due to vote shift than to vote concentration but there is an element of capriciousness.

As a result of its inherent "top-heaviness", the Smiley reform seems more likely to result in majority governments, at least in the short run. Over a longer term, strong regional parties could arise and negate this effect. Because it does reward at least some second place finishes, the Smiley proposal has weaker barriers against new entrants than does a plurality system, but stronger ones than my own proposal.

The Smiley reform *will* stimulate strong local campaigns. Indeed, it may overshoot the mark in this by inducing candidates from the traditional parties to depart from their party platform in ways more appealing to local interests. In areas of weakness for one major party, Quebec for the Conservatives and the Prairies for the Liberals, the weak party will not be competing with its major party rival for constituency seats — these are too far out of reach — but with the local third parties for the provincial seats. This too might lead to a campaign different from the national campaign. The incentive, under the Smiley proposal, to depart from the national campaign, would be no stronger than under the present plurality system, but would be greater than under the proposal made in the previous section. In that system, constituency candidates would always keep an eye on party preferment — on seeking a favourable spot on their party's list.

The absence of a list also means that the Smiley proposal offers no capacity for the development of political careers. Though a party might be able to retain a relatively stable proportion of provincial seats, the candidates actually filling these could change at each election. In years of strong third party emergence, a provincial seat might be won with 40% or less of a constituency vote, with the second place finisher having only one-third of the vote. If the third party subsequently collapses, the provincial member could increase his vote to 43% and find that he loses his seat because other second place finishers managed to raise their vote to 45%. He would be a casualty of the already noted capriciousness of the system.

In summary, the Smiley proposal differs from the one in this monograph in the degree of the proportionality among parties in the final outcome, in the extent to which it allows party caucuses to reflect the national distribution of the party vote, and in affording parties the opportunity to develop political careers for provincial spokesmen. As a result of these effects, the Smiley proposal increases the likelihood of majority government as compared with more strictly proportional schemes which would vitually guarantee that no party had a majority of parliamentary seats.

B. The Broadbent Proposal

On July 27, 1968, the leader of the NDP, Ed Broadbent, proposed in the House of Commons that the Senate be abolished and that the House of Commons be enlarged by 100 seats. Unlike Donald Smiley, Broadbent abandoned representation by population for these seats, seeking instead to have 20 allocated to each of five regions: British Columbia, the Prairies, Ontario, Quebec and the Atlantic region. Regional representatives were to be apportioned among the parties according to their percentage share of the regional vote. Broadbent proposed to fill the seats by the regional list method, but the Smiley method would also be a possibility. However, the first would be superior in terms of career development. Under the Broadbent proposals, the *number* of each party's seats in each region would be independent of the spatial distribution of the votes within the regions. Were the occupant of each seat to be selected by the Smiley method, then the occupant's length of service would depend on local factors.

The Broadbent proposal can be criticized for its abandonment of representation by population, though this is not inherent in the proposal. One could only justify abandoning this principle by the claim that regional interests are distinct on virtually all matters of public policy and that the alienation of the less populous regions is traceable to their relative weakness in parliament. Neither proposition would withstand critical examination. There may be grounds for requiring qualified majorities on certain items of public policy, but not for over-representing certain regions on all issues. The regions specified are themselves internally homogeneous only on a limited public policy agenda. Moreover, power in parliament is no longer as important as it once was. Far more important is representation in the caucus of the governing party. Because the Broadbent proposal gives seats to parties in their strong, as well as in their weak, regions, it does not achieve as satisfactory a balance among regions in party caucuses as does the proposal in this monograph.

Nothing in the process of allocating the additional seats stimulates local campaigning. In their traditionally weak regions, parties may well prefer media campaigns, concentrated on the region's largest urban media markets, to local door-knocking. This is made even more probable by the inherent "stickiness" of dividing 20 seats up into whole numbers. Although the precise allocation of seats will depend on the exact distribution of votes among the parties, 42.51% of the regional vote would likely be as productive of seats as would 47.49%. In each region, therefore, a party could fall almost five percentage points short of its potential vote at virtually no cost in regional seats. In weak regions, constituency success is so far from attainable that maximum constituency effort is not required for those seats either, so that party organization development gets less stimulation than under other systems.

One cannot forecast how the Broadbent proposal would affect the likelihood of majority government. No party would have a majority of that part of the House of Commons (100 seats in the Broadbent reform) which is allocated proportionately. Whether or not a party gains an absolute majority depends on the extent to which the plurality system has exaggerated the party's constituency strength. In 1974, the Liberals would have won 42 regional seats in the original Broadbent version and would have had a one-seat parliamentary majority instead of the eight-seat majority actually obtained. In that year, the plurality system had exaggerated Liberal seat strength by 23%, a not unusual rate for majority-producing elections. Elections like that of 1972, which result in minority governments under the present system, would result in minority governments under these Smiley and Broadbent proposals. They are thus somewhat less likely to result in minority governments than this proposal.

C. National Seats with d'Hondt Divisors

Although not part of public debate, the following scheme has been devised in the spirit of the previous ones but more deliberately focussed on reinforcing parties in those provinces where the plurality system exacts its sternest penalties. Under the two previous proposals in this subsection, the operation of proportionality is circumscribed. It applies only to a portion of the total parliamentary seats. As a result, the proposals have the advantage, at least in the views of some people, of minimizing the chances of minority government while making parties more representative of all regions. However, under these proposals, some of the "compensatory" seats are nonetheless allocated to parties in their strongest regions: the Liberals in Quebec, the Progressive Conservatives on the Prairies. This seems wasteful. The additional seats are meant, in all proposals, to enable parties to get spokesmen from regions where constituencies are hard to win despite a sizeable aggregate vote. Focussing the seats better on this objective would not necessarily make minority government more probable than would the other "additional seats" proposals examined in this section.

Under the system of national seats, the pool is divided among the parties according to their national percentages of the popular vote. Once it has been determined how many seats each party is to get, the seats are allocated among provinces in the following way:

1. the party vote in each province is divided by $n+1$, where n is the number of seats won by the party in each province;
2. the party vote in each province is successively divided by a sequence of integers, $n+2, n+3, \ldots n+p$, where p is the total number of seats allocated to the party;
3. the quotients from the divisions are rank ordered from highest to lowest, and the p largest quotients identify the provinces to which seats are given.

An example of this count, allocating 100 seats based on the 1974 election results, is given in Appendix B. The actual identity of those to occupy the seats could come, preferably, from provincial lists. A province where the Liberals were entitled to 5 seats would give those to the top five names on the Liberal list for that province, skipping over names of people already elected. The allocation could follow the Smiley method as well, and give the seats to the party's top vote-getters in each province. Again, this would limit the capacity of political parties to develop political careers in each province.

Table 8 shows the allocation of additional seats by party and region in 1974, assuming all other outcomes in that election to have remained the

Table 8

Distribution of 100 Additional Seats by Party and Region in 1974
under Four Hypothetical Allocation Systems

	Atlantic	Quebec	Ontario	Prairies	B.C.	Total
LIBERAL						
Irvine	6	0	1	10	3	20
Smiley	6	11	19	7	1	44
Broadbent	9	11	9	6	7	42
National-d'Hondt*	5	1	20	12	6	44
PROG. CONS.						
Irvine	1	16	19	0	1	37
Smiley	4	11	14	5	6	40
Broadbent	9	4	7	10	8	38
National-d'Hondt	0	15	19	0	2	36
NEW DEM. PARTY						
Irvine	3	6	16	6	6	37
Smiley	0	0	3	4	3	10
Broadbent	2	1	4	4	5	16
National-d'Hondt	0	3	7	2	3	15
SOCIAL CREDIT						
Irvine	0	6	0	0	0	6
Smiley	0	6	0	0	0	6
Broadbent	0	4	0	0	0	4
National-d'Hondt	0	5	0	0	0	5
TOTAL						
Irvine	10	28	36	16	10	100
Smiley	10	28	36	16	10	100
Broadbent	20	20	20	20	20	100
National-d'Hondt	5	24	46	14	11	100

* National seats allocated among provinces by the d'Hondt counting system.

same, and assuming that the additional seats were simply added on to the existing 264 seats in the House of Commons. All systems would have given the Progressive Conservative party virtually the same number of seats. The Smiley proposal would have been somewhat more favourable to that party, and the "National Seat + d'Hondt" system would have been least favourable. The system proposed in this monograph is much less favourable to the Liberals in aggregate and much more favourable to the NDP than any other dual representation system — including the one proposed by Ed Broadbent! This would always be true for the leading party, and it is for that reason that the Irvine proposal is so much more likely to produce minority governments. The other three systems treat the Liberals in substantially the same fashion in aggregate, and give the most popular party the largest share of the second tier of seats. Of the three systems reviewed in this subsection, Professor Smiley's is least favourable to the NDP in aggregate, while the Broadbent and the "National Seats" methods would have treated the NDP in equivalent fashion.

Turning from the aggregate allocation of seats to its distribution, we see that the proposal in this monograph is indeed efficient in enabling parties to strengthen representation from the areas where they do most poorly under plurality rules. Under that system, the Liberals get 13 seats west of Ontario — 65% of the total Liberal allocation. Only the "National Seats" proposal gives more to the Liberals in the West, but that is because the total allocation is larger. Under the "National Seats" + d'Hondt" method, 42% of the Liberal allocation would go to Liberal lists in the west. The Irvine proposal also treats the Progressive Conservatives and the NDP most generously in Quebec, though the "National Seats" system gives a higher proportion of the NDP's allocation to Quebec than does the Irvine proposal.

Of the systems least likely to produce minority governments, the "National Seats + d'Hondt" system is the most efficient with respect to compensating for the effects of the plurality system. Both absolutely and proportionately, this system gives more seats to a party's poorest region and fewest to its best regions. The Liberals get only one seat in Quebec, the Progressive Conservatives none on the Prairies. This system has two drawbacks, however.

First, it leads to a final allocation of seats which is disproportionate to population. Although it does not depart from "representation by population" as seriously as the Broadbent proposal does, it would, in 1974, have underrepresented the Atlantic region by 5 seats (in a 364-seat House this equals underrepresentation of 1.4%); Quebec by 4 seats (-1.1%); and the Prairies by 2 seats (-0.5%). B.C. would have been slightly overrepresented (+0.3% = 1 seat) and Ontario substantially so (by 10 seats = 2.7%). This pattern would not be fixed, but would depend on the election results. We would always expect some departure from strict representation by population. The magnitude of that departure could be lessened by having fewer second tier seats. Given the greater efficiency of this method, one could allocate only 60 seats, of which 9 would go to Prairie Liberals, 5 to B.C. Liberals and 11 to Quebec Conservatives. A 60-seat second tier in 1974 would have underrepresented the Atlantic region by 1% to the benefit of Ontario.

A more serious objection is the reliance of the system on *national* vote percentages. Not only does this not encourage local campaigns, it does not even require parties to campaign seriously in areas of weakness. In 1974, the Liberals got just over 400,000 votes on the Prairies. If a certain policy line offered itself with the prospect of gaining 250,000 votes in the east at the loss of 200,000 votes in the west, the party should presumably opt for such a policy. There are, of course, many factors which stop parties from such cold-blooded calculation, not the least of which would be the strengthened position of regional spokesmen in the party caucus. Broader representation provides an opportunity for party building but does not in itself provide the incentive. An electoral system of allocating national seats by the d'Hondt system would provide no more incentive to party-building throughout the country than does the present electoral system. That should be condemnation enough.

Recent Canadian proposals for the reform of the electoral system all involve two levels of representation: constituencies on the one hand, provinces or regions on the other. No proposal is willing to totally abandon the single-member constituency system which is so much a part of our tradition and which can serve to keep MPs attentive to constituents. Some dual representation systems are more efficient than others in overcoming the effects of the plurality system, and each has consequences other than this primary one. The additional consequences are viewed differently by different people, but no system would evoke unanimous approval. For these refinements of the dual representation system, as for the larger choice among types of electoral system, the tradeoff is between more faithful representation of the vote and governments needing the support of more than one party. The next section of this monograph will focus again on this choice.

6 Would the Proposed System Do What We Want?

Although this monograph has, at various points, made reference to the Canadian scene, the argument has had a certain free-floating quality. The case for a new electoral system has been put in terms of effects (or non-effects) on various general values as if these were, in themselves, sufficient to carry the day. Reform is unlikely, however, unless it can be shown to be in the interests, whether immediate or as they might evolve in the short term, of current political actors. Moreover, reform is undesirable, in that it would constitute no more than a distraction, unless it can be shown that the reform would meet some pressing problem.

It takes no great theoretical insight or act of imagination to predict that Canadian politics will be marked by increasing conflict. Even before November 15th, 1976 one might have made such a forecast. The tremendous increase in the price of energy in 1973 introduced a new element to the world economy which could not be quickly absorbed through traditional means. The growing sluggishness of the western economies has had profound effects on a Canada dependent on strong foreign demand for its raw materials. The fuel crisis stimulated industrial economies with no energy resources, Japan for example, to compete even more vigorously in world markets — thus confronting Canadian manufacturers within Canada, as well as abroad. Finally, the fuel crisis sharpened internal conflicts — between Alberta and Saskatchewan on the one hand and energy-consuming provinces on the other, and, possibly more intensely in the future, between Inuit and southerners.

One response of the leading Western economic powers to the fuel crisis has been to convene a new round of negotiation on world tariff and other trade barriers. The objective of the stronger industrial nations is to enhance the free flow of both manufactured goods and raw materials. This too will enhance the clash of economic interests within Canada. With the election of the *Parti Québécois* a new dimension of conflict was added to the economic ones then brewing. The renegotiation of the relationship between Quebec and the rest of Canada complicates the economic problems by confounding them, at least partially, with the cultural goals and fears of French-Quebeckers. This introduces less "bargainable" dimensions and results in an easy, if largely spurious, concretization of economic issues. It makes it all too likely that economic frustration can be attributed to the "imperialism" of English Canadians or to the lack of patriotism of French-Canadians. The potential thus exists for a much more overtly racist party politics than has marked Canadian politics in recent years.

As was evident in the emotional power released by the air traffic control dispute of 1976, a politics centered on ethnic conflict makes Canada virtually ungovernable. A system of proportional representation would help to defuse any such conflict not supported by majorities in both English and French Canada. The leadership of both the Liberal and Progressive Conservative parties recognize this.

In a period of high potential racism, a more proportional representation system would be a double-edged sword. In the short run, it would represent new racist movements whether these were staffed by dissident members of established parties or by people wholly new to Canadian politics. Moreover, it would represent these immediately where one might assume that the present electoral system, buttressed perhaps by a prime minister's good sense of timing, would delay their emergence. Certainly the analysis of Table 4 showed that the present party system provides only a weak barrier to such new parties.

One must not unduly exaggerate this threat, however. Although it is impossible to generalize the results of Table 4 to a context where there actually were new competitors, the most extreme scenario suggests that present parties could hold on to half their voting strength in each region, and probably considerably more than that in the Atlantic Provinces and Ontario. Since the extremist movements will be extreme in a regionalist sense, one can assume that their activity will not be coordinated and that they will not make simultaneous breakthroughs in all parts of the country. Consider the following scenario of the most unfavourable consequences under a new electoral system:

1. a separatist French Canadian party gains half the Quebec seats in the first election under dual representation;
2. a western Canadian separatist party gains half the western seats in the second election under a new system, after having gained one-quarter the seats in the first election;
3. racist English Canadian parties gain one-third of the seats in the Atlantic region and Ontario by the third election with other new parties holding their strength.

Professor Hermens rightly stressed that one of the greatest threats to a democratic system comes when the extremist parties can monopolize the opposition. This occurs when a government can only be sustained by a coalition of all the centrist parties (Hermens, 1941, pp. 27-30). Would Canada get to that point under the above scenario? It certainly does not after the first election under dual representation. About 70 of 354 seats are held by two extremist parties. This is 20% of the whole parliament, and less than half the opposition. By the end of the second election, about 27% of the whole House is lost to new forces. While this constitutes more than half the opposition, it is divided approximately equally in two so that the largest opposition party is still one of the established parties. By the end of the third election, another 33 seats are lost to extremist fragments. By now, the system is approaching the state envisaged by Professor Hermens. However, the approach would have been much more rapid under the present system. In 1974, the Liberals received 54% of the Quebec vote and got a 50% bonus in seats. Applying the same bonus in our scenario, the new separatist party would be getting 75% of the 94 seats or about 70 seats. It is true that only about one-eighth of the western seats would be lost, but it means that more than 80 seats would be held by extremist forces after the first election. By the time of the second election, we have posited the separatist tendencies to be stronger in the west than the Progressive Conservative party was in 1974, when it won 47% of the vote in the four western provinces and 63% of the western seats. Applying the same bonus to the new forces would give them two-thirds of the western seats. In all, about 132 seats would be held by extremist forces after the second election. Thus, the perilous state is reached in two elections under plurality but three under dual representation — all, admittedly, under a fairly extreme scenario.

The general point is that only when new forces get less than one-third of the vote are PR systems more fragile than plurality electoral systems. But if new forces *are* that weak, and also uncoordinated nationally, they can easily be excluded from government and are unlikely to have sufficient parliamentary power to be too disruptive, even under PR. Under plurality, their exclusion would be even more complete, but this seems to be overkill when considered in the light of the costs imposed on established parties by a plurality electoral system.

To see minority or coalition government as inevitable under a new electoral system is not to say that the new parliament will therefore be unworkable. The main beneficiary of any change would be the NDP, if benefit is measured in terms of numbers of seats, and the major parties, if benefit is measured in terms of the nationalization of the caucus. Even if the NDP were unable to improve on its 15.4% of the 1974 vote, its seats in the enlarged parliament would number 55. Its gain under the worst possible assumption would match the gain of Quebec or western separatist parties under the most favourable assumptions. The likelihood, especially for the first election after a change of electoral system, is that class-based politics would be strengthened and not that fragmentation and extremism would ensue.

But why should the Liberals or Progressive Conservatives want to change the electoral system? Liberals have done very well by the current system in this country. The Progressive Conservatives may prefer to gamble that their turn will come to be big winners rather than to accept the certainty of only a proportionate share of seats. Moreover, the balance of interests in each party would seem against it. Because of the design of the proposal, few sitting members would in fact lose seats, but, relatively, the proposal does ask Quebec Liberals to give up seats to Conservatives and New Democrats, and asks western Conservatives to give place to Liberals and New Democrats.

One of the major contentions of Cairns' original analysis of the present electoral system was precisely that parties would be most sensitive to interests expressed by MPs from areas where the party did best (Cairns, 1968). Lovink challenged this on grounds that there was no evidence bearing on the matter and that one could make a logical case for the opposite behaviour (Lovink, 1970). It is a pleasant irony to think that electoral system reform might itself be a crucial test between the two positions. Cairns would expect little enthusiasm for such reform; Lovink might be more sanguine about the possibility for reform. The burden of my preceeding analysis of the susceptibility of the party system to a new kind of party suggests, however, that national party leaders may not have any choice about whether or not they are going to lose strength. Even in their best areas, parties are sufficiently weakly rooted that they might not be able to withstand an extremist party. While they might be able to move to capture some of the extremist vote, their freedom of mobility could be limited by the unwillingness of leaders to change their platforms radically or by the inability of the parties to do so credibly.

However, given the way parties define their interests, only a clear threat to the current system is likely to induce them to venture on this kind of reform. Given that it was so easy, in 1973, to persuade oneself that separatism was dead, it will not be easy to convince federal party leaders of the fragility of their electoral support. Those benefitting from the current system find it difficult to accept that it could turn against them — until the morning after it has happened. Political scientists need not, and should not, carry the same tune through the same graveyard.

What would it take to put electoral system reform higher on the

Canadian political agenda? The following situations could be crucial:

1. a sustained period of minority government;
2. the NDP holding the balance of power;
3. substantial erosion of the Liberal vote in Quebec by third parties;
4. a heightened English/French polarization in the House of Commons.

A sustained period of minority government in Canada would be further proof of the Liberals' inability to win seats in the west, and of the Progressive Conservative party's inability to make a breakthrough in central Canada. The latter term is used deliberately since Conservative weakness in Ontario may be a result of their perceived inability to win seats in Quebec and to effectively mediate current conflicts. While there are substantial reasons for both failures, they are exacerbated by the electoral system. The Progressive Conservatives might be induced to accept reform simply to rid itself of the stigma of being unable to get a strong Quebec caucus.

As we have seen, the NDP has shown some interest in electoral system reform. They would clearly benefit from almost any change, and would benefit most from the dual representation system. A prolonged period of minority government might put the NDP in a decisive position if it can monopolize the protest vote. If NDP votes were crucial to sustaining a government, the party might choose to make some kind of electoral system reform part of the price of support.

The NDP might not be the only swing party in parliament. There could be other territorially concentrated parties. Social Credit in Quebec may again rise Phoenix-like from the ashes of newspaper obituaries. Even more nationalist parties such as the *Union Populaire* could also win a number of seats. Such parties would have little interest in electoral system reform. They might even benefit from the present system. They would pose such a threat to the electoral base of the Liberal party, however, that that party would turn to electoral system reform as a way of blunting the third party attack. Huge majorities in Montreal could not block the *Créditistes* under the present electoral system but could help to preserve the Liberal party under a dual representation system.

Finally, it is possible that the situation might require political parties to rise above self-interest. Canada has had many shocks recently, and more are likely. The air traffic control dispute and the election of the *Parti Québécois* in 1976, may well be followed in 1979 by a federal government with few French Canadian members and an ambiguous Quebec referendum which appears to strengthen the PQ. One hopes that this is not the situation which precipitates electoral system reform. However, such reform would be the most effective and visible short-term response in a crisis atmosphere. It is clearly within the competence of the federal government and would immediately bring better representation of all parts of Canada to both sides of the House of Commons.

These lines are written at the very beginning of the 1979 federal election campaign. All, some, or none of the above scenarios are possible at this stage. What one can firmly predict at this stage is that the 1979 parliament will be as unrepresentative as all its predecessors. Even if the actual outcome does not make electoral system reform immediately attractive, the four conditions just listed remain possibilities for future elections.

Whether or not parliamentary conditions favoured electoral system reform, it is often claimed that Canadians have a visceral reaction against minority or coalition government as something undesirable and un-Canadian (Cairns, 1968, pp. 55-6). Such sentiment does show up in response to direct questions on opinion surveys. In 1965, 57% felt the issue of minority government to be very important and 61% felt that whether or not one had a majority government made a great deal of difference. Nine years later, in 1974, 55% still said that they preferred majority government as opposed to 28% preferring minority government. There is some contrary evidence, however. In 1973, 54% felt that minority government had been good for the nation, and very few volunteered the matter one way or another to very general and open-ended questions asking about election concerns. Moreover, the salience of the issue appeared to decline between 1965 and 1974: 48% in the former year but only 28% in the latter professed to be "very likely" or "fairly likely" to switch parties to obtain a majority (Leduc, 1977, pp. 314-5). The actual impact of the issue was probably less than that. Many voters do not act on professed intentions: others profess intentions consistent with what they would do on other grounds anyway. While one cannot assess the degree to which the issue prevents party switching that otherwise would have occurred, net benefit to the Liberal party declined from 1.1% in 1965 to 0.2% in 1974 among those who voted both in those elections and the preceeding one. Among those first entering the electorate in 1965 and 1974 and professing the issue to be a salient one, the net benefit to Liberals was 1.3% in 1965 and 1.7% in 1974. (For more detail, see Leduc's careful study, 1977).

The particular proposal put forward in this monograph could also fall afoul of an "anti-party" tradition in the west and could be viewed as a further device to achieve the subordination of western to central Canadian interests. With equal polemical fervour, if not equal traditional prejudice, our system could be dismissed by Quebec nationalists as a device to recruit "vendus" to the caucuses of all the federal parties.

73

Though the question was not designed specifically to tap evaluations of parties, we should recall from Table 4 that westerners were, if anything, *more* likely to feel that it made a difference which party formed the government. Whatever the strength of the tradition, our proposal is aimed against neither Quebec nor the west. Either would have the option of supporting new parties if they found that they could not work effectively through established parties. The point is that their interests are better served by *parties*. Parties are instruments for popular power in a way that single candidates contesting primaries or capturing particular constituencies cannot be. It is for this reason that we have argued against the modifications of proportionality which would diminish the incentives to party-building.

While survey results do not suggest overwhelming popular opposition, we must remember that tradition is embodied not only in popular feelings but also in the structures of parliamentary government and constitutional monarchy. Coalition government is more compatible with the traditions of parliamentary government than is minority government. When one party seeks to govern alone with less than half the seats, there is always the temptation to fudge the meaning of a defeat in parliament. Instead, the life of a government is made to depend on an explicit vote of confidence. A coalition government, unless it is composed of the barest of majorities, should not lose a parliamentary vote unless the coalition itself has been strained to the breaking point. Lost votes are stronger signals to government than they are under minority governments. They may indicate the inability of the government to continue and will always lead to the resignation of the government. One must not read into this the re-establishment of parliamentary supremacy. As always, the life of a government will be the prerogative of political leadership, though "leaderships" becomes the appropriate term under proportional representation.

With electoral reform, it is likely that we would have coalitions rather than minority government. Of the 17 elections since 1921, only 9 resulted in any party getting at least 45% of the national vote. With new actors, and greater encouragement to vote NDP (since one's vote would not be "wasted"), it is highly unlikely that any party would get more than 40% of the vote, and hence 40% of the seats, under the proposed system. Though both major parties have achieved upwards of 45% in the past, the analysis of Table 4 suggested that only 60 to 75% of this support is secure. A long-run possibility is that major party strength would settle down in the 25% range, the more popular one being somewhat higher in any election, the other somewhat lower. At this level, two-party coalition governments would appear quite viable, though a major party might also choose to govern with a larger number of smaller regional parties.

74

Depending on how difficult it was to make and to maintain coalitions, a more proportional system could have implications for constitutional monarchy in Canada. Many new questions would be raised, each with implications for the office of Governor-General. How much time would a party be allowed in its attempt to form a government? Would a coalition defeated in parliament be allowed a dissolution of parliament? Under what conditions? Would the defeated prime minister be allowed to try to reconstitute a government before a coalition-building mandate was offered to another party leader? In the latter case, which one — one involved in the last government or not? With so much discretion in the hands of the chief executive, it could become increasingly unacceptable that he should be an appointed official. This is quite apart from the issue of whether we want to have as chief executive someone who is formally representative of the Queen. It is clear, however, that an elected chief executive would be a representative of the electorate. Canada could, of course, remain part of the Commonwealth as other republics have done. Moreover, it does not necessarily follow from PR that Canada must have a republic. So long as there is clearly one most popular party, and so long as it can form a coalition that can survive for about four years, the designation of the prime minister will appear as routine as it does now. If the chief executive's formal discretion is circumscribed in fact, there should be little question about his status.

Are coalition governments good or bad? Clearly there can be no single answer since there are many different dimensions of evaluation. We have already reviewed some of the evidence dealing with the policy-making capacity of such governments. In Canadian history, we have had two experiences of coalitions seeking explicit policy objectives. The first was to establish Confederation itself, where virtually all the constituent units (except Canada East) saw coalitions between men who had been quite bitter enemies: Macdonald and Brown in Canada West; Smith, Wilmot and Tilley in New Brunswick; Tupper, Archibald and later Joseph Howe in Nova Scotia. Cooperation between Brown and Macdonald ended after Confederation was accomplished but the other "colleagues" stayed together, a phenomenon much aided by federal government patronage. The second such coalition — the Union Government of 1917 joining some English-speaking Liberals to the previous Conservative government — would now be rated as a much less attractive example. Its aim was to impose conscription on a reluctant rural population, most of which was French-speaking but also including many new immigrants and was marked by blatant manipulation of the franchise. Because Canada outside Quebec was not united against French Quebeckers, this coalition was neither widespread nor a long-lasting mobilization of English versus French, but it did mark a watershed in the relations between French Canadians and the Conservative party with all the implications that has for national unity. Electoral reform proposals are, in good part, attempts to moderate the continuing consequences of the 1917 coalition.

Each of these coalitions had definite implications for the relative strengths of political parties in some regions, but neither completely undermined political forces. Pre-coalition lines generally re-emerged after the first bloom was off the coalition experience. The same cannot be said for coalitions at the provincial level. Putting aside instances of cooperation between the Liberal and Progressive parties, and that between Quebec Conservatives and the ALN which are better characterized as "absorptions" where one partner did not have a long-established identity, there have been two coalitions in provincial politics: Liberals and Conservatives in British Columbia from 1941 to 1952, and the Liberal-Progressive party with the Conservatives in Manitoba from 1940 to 1950. In both cases, the rationale seems to have been the necessity to block the CCF. Both coalitions must be rated unsuccessful from the standpoint of the institutional interests of at least one of the partners. In British Columbia, both the Liberals and the Progressive Conservatives have had virtually no provincial existence since 1952. In the Manitoba case, the Progressive Conservatives were able to build a provincial party after pulling out of the coalition but the Liberals have been decimated since the late 1950's.

European and Canadian federal experience suggests that coalition is not necessarily so fatal to parties as institutions. Indeed, the most common charge is that parties are motivated to become too distinct. In the B.C. and Manitoba cases, two other forces were at work: the anti-party ideological tradition of western small businessmen which was almost as strong as their anti-leftism; and the competing institutional needs of the federal counterparts to these parties. The conjunction of these forces meant that the coalition partners had neither the motivation nor the resources to build strong parties (Whitaker, 1977). One should not extrapolate from these cases that, were a more proportional electoral system introduced, subsequent coalition governments would be swept away by new political actors. The cases do remind us, however, that changing the electoral system at only one level of a federal state would be another force motivating federal and provincial wings of the same nominal party to establish separate organizations and sources of financing, and perhaps distinct names as well. This trend is now so well established that the situation can be seen as facilitating electoral system reform at the federal level rather than seeing such reform as having undesirable new consequences.

In a formal sense, coalition government would seem highly desirable in Canada. A large measure of the current alienation from federal government comes from the fact that its formal power exceeds its real social power. Governments act, and must act, on behalf of the whole country but they do not have support from a majority of the voters, nor do they have caucus representation from large segments of the society. Coalition governments would be more broadly based both numerically and in terms of the variety of interests to which the partners would be responsive. This would certainly increase the difficulties of government formation, but Canada *is* a difficult country to govern and it is unwise to mask this artificially. It is worth complicating the bargaining process if the bargains are thereby more acceptable. The negotiation process would not be public, but parties would have to publicly defend their agreements and this too would help overcome some of the political alienation in the country. Governing programmes would have greater weight than they now do when the bargaining is informal and intra-party. Coalition governments with commitments to some sector — western shippers or urban commuters — would not be able to stall action on these commitments as readily as a single party government can do. Coalitions are more representative than single partly majorities and more formal than bargains concluded by a minority government and therefore stronger than both.

At the same time, we must recognize that the impact of representative institutions, such as parties, parliaments or cabinets on government is low in modern societies — in Canada as well as elsewhere. Making the above institutions more representative is only ultimately effective if they can also be made more powerful. This has also been a theme in the appraisal of electoral systems. The focus, however, has been on the party outside parliament — on how to build it up and give it impact over parliamentarians. A multi-party government would multiply the number of skeptical eyes cast over advice forthcoming from the professional civil service and, one hopes, over the less savoury actions of public servants. However, this is no substitute for other reforms designed to increase the information available to parliamentarians. One could imagine a whole host of parliamentary committee reforms to achieve this end and to offer a role to the groups excluded for the moment from government.

It is important that we be clear about the alternatives. Whatever the future constitutional developments, it is inconceivable that the point would ever be reached where no central policy affects the units that now constitute Canada. That being the case, the issue is how that policy is to be made. We may have already passed the point where that policy can be made by other than professional civil servants — whether these meet as they do now, or as ambassadors of states as sovereign as any can be nowadays. The real value of strengthening parliaments is that these make policy relatively openly. They cannot dispense with expert advice. It is quite conceivable that a coalition could develop as trusting and unquestioning a relationship with its advisers as the Liberal government now has. However, insofar as the parties have a need for a strong extra-parliamentary wing, they will be unable to focus quite so much attention on their civil service advisers as they do at present.

We mustn't be too sanguine about this development, however. The most proportional parliaments coexist with the most elaborate corporatist structures. These may be viewed as a kind of functional federalism wherein certain decisions, for reasons of timing or acceptability (Lehmbruch, 1977), are left to bodies whose composition is independent of the election returns. Although the more pressing conflicts in Canada have been between cultures and regions rather than immediately between economic groups, these conflicts too have often been devolved onto non-elected bodies for settlement. Given the growing bureaucratization of federal and provincial governments, and the technical nature of the conflicts, this trend will probably not be halted in the near future. Inter-bureaucratic working sessions will necessarily precede bargaining among political executives and these may tend to do little more than ratify agreements struck elsewhere.

While this is probably quite independent of any change in systems of representation, it does seem plausible that a more broadly based political executive, especially one with responsibilities to party organizations, may insist on a broader role for itself. Only one of the causes of the decline of representative institutions is that they are not representative enough. They are also not well enough informed and not efficient enough in their use of time. However, representativeness may be crucial. If the political parties can be induced, by electoral system reform and other reforms, to work at organizing their supporters and representing them (rather than gambling on general swings of contentment and discontent) part of the problem will have been tackled. Under a more proportional system, many of the politicians would have assured careers *as politicians* without at the same time having assured careers as governors. As a result, parliamentarians may develop perspectives and interests distinct from those of the public service and would therefore be motivated to seek out tools to enhance their capacity for control.

Controlling the bureaucratic state is our long term problem. Producing parliamentary parties and governments able to reflect the diversity of the country is our immediate one. The contribution of electoral system reform to solving this is unquestionable. The simulation of the 1974 election under the system of dual representation showed the likely consequences: a government with seventeen members from the Prairies, and an official opposition with twenty members from Quebec. This, or something like it, is what would occur under a reformed system of allocating seats in parliament. The party system would not fragment in the short run. It need not in the long run and certainly need not produce unworkable parliaments. By assuring better representativeness to our parliamentary parties, a reformed electoral system would accomplish two things:

1. elections would no longer imply the virtual exclusion of Quebec or of the west from power;
2. interests which can now only make themselves heard through provincial governments, if at all, would find they had increased weight in Ottawa. These at least are prerequisite to revitalizing the central government and harnessing it to serve the common interests of Canadians.

Appendix A
Types of
Electoral System

Our present electoral system is a plurality system such as currently exists in Britain and the United States for election to the lower house of their legislature. Those who wish to run for the House of Commons present themselves in a territorially defined constituency which will be represented by one Member of Parliament. The MP will be the one who obtains more of the votes cast at the election than does any other candidate. Voting proceeds by making a mark, usually an "X", on a ballot paper opposite the name of the candidate which the voter wishes to support. No specified percentage of the total vote has to be obtained in order to win. Where there are more than two candidates to represent the constituency, it will quite often be the case that the winner will have less than half the votes cast.

A close relation to this system is the alternative vote AV system, which is used to elect the lower house of the Australian legislature. Here, again, constituencies are represented by a single member of parliament chosen from among many candidates. In this system, however, voters are encouraged not to make a single mark on the ballot paper, but to indicate their degree of preference among candidates. They put "1" opposite the name of their most preferred candidate, "2" opposite the one they like next best, and so on. Variants of this system arise from the degree of encouragement to fill out the whole ballot. In Australia, a ballot is deemed spoiled unless a virtually complete rank ordering is made by the voter (Jaensch, 1975). This is not a necessary feature of the system, and we could allow the voter to stop indicating preferences whenever he chooses. The object of this system is to elect that candidate who is ultimately viewed as "closest" to themselves (in some sort of preference space which may be defined by issues: voters may like all the positions

Table A1

A Hypothetical Constituency Count Under an AV Electoral System

Candidate	First Count	Second Count	Third Count	Fourth Count
Mr. White	7424	7624	7724	—
Ms. Green	5732	6232	7732	9732
Mr. Brown	2638	3538	—	—
Ms. Black	1976	—	—	—
Mr. Scarlett	6146	6346	7746	9246
TOTAL	23,916	23,740	23,202	18,978
Non-transferable		176	538	4224

taken by their first candidate, most of those taken by the second, etc.). Counting of the votes proceeds as in Table A1, starting with the first preferences. Should a candidate receive more first preferences than all other candidates combined, he (or she) would be declared elected and counting would stop. In the hypothetical example of Table A1, Mr. White had the highest number of votes, but still under one-third of the total cast. He would, nonetheless, have been declared elected under a plurality system. Under AV, the candidate with the fewest first preferences is eliminated, and his vote redistributed according to his second preferences. In this example, 176 of Ms. Black's voters indicated no further preferences, 900 gave Mr. Brown as their second preference, 400 went to Ms. Green and 200 each to Mr. White and Mr. Scarlett. Although Mr. Brown was the biggest beneficiary from the redistribution, he remains the least preferred candidate still in the race and so is dropped for the third count. The *next available* preferences of his voters are distributed. In the case of the vote he got from Ms. Black, these will be third preferences. Similarly, some of his voters will list Ms. Black as their second preference. She being eliminated, these votes are distributed according to their third preferences. Since many voters will not have indicated second or third preferences, I have assumed a further 538 ballots to be non-transferable. The 3,000 that can be distributed make the race very close indeed, but Mr. White is eliminated. For the sake of discussion, I have assumed that most of his voters cared for no other candidate. Perhaps he really was M. Leblanc or Sig. Bianco and his supporters cared only to express group solidarity, not to choose among others. In any case, those 2,500 who do indicate a further preference split marginally towards

Ms. Green and she is declared elected. Note that she does not have support from half of the original 23,916 voters, though she does have more than half of the votes of those who are still not indifferent by the fourth ballot. Whether or not she really occupies a midpoint in a "space"of voter sentiment would require a philosopical and empirical inquiry into the meaning of the unwillingness to declare further preferences. If this arises from true indifference then we might suppose that, were everyone obliged to declare a full preference ordering, all would do so randomly among the candidates to which they were indifferent, and Ms. Green has a good claim to representing the majority preference of all voters. Non-transferability arising from ignorance or alienation would be a different matter.

A third type of electoral system — the "two-ballot" system, used for legislative and presidential elections in France for example, is akin to the previous two. Like both of these, a constituency is represented by a single member of parliament. As with the plurality system, the voter simply makes a mark against the name of the candidate he wishes to support (and, on the first ballot, this is probably the one he most prefers). Like the AV system, a candidate is declared elected on the first round only if he is preferred by a majority of the voters. If no one is preferred by a majority on the first count, a second election is held, usually a week later. In France, only very weak candidates are obliged to withdraw from the race, and the victor on the second ballot is the one with a plurality of the vote. In effect, the French system is a combination of the American nomination-by-primary-election and a plurality electoral system for the final choice. One could oblige all but the top two candidates to withdraw from the contest before the second ballot, and then the winning candidate *a fortiori* represents a majority of those who turn out on the second ballot.

Like the problem of non-transferability, many will not vote on the second ballot because they are indifferent (positively or negatively) between the remaining contestants. Had the hypothetical constituency of Table A1 been using a two-ballot system with compulsory withdrawal, only Messrs. White and Scarlet would have remained in the contest, and one cannot guess who might have won since the preferences of Ms. Green's supporters are unknown. Had Mr. White's supporters' relative preference for her been reciprocated, he probably would have won under a two-ballot system. If there were no compulsory withdrawal, Ms. Green might still have won if only Ms. Black dropped out, and Mr. Scarlett might have won if he could persuade both Black and Brown to leave the way clear. Although I know of no study of the question, it is probable that the turnout declines between the two ballots are much larger in magnitude than non-transferability in an AV system. Hence it is hazardous to speculate on the eventual winner under a two-ballot system of a first count situation as depicted in Table A1, though it may be noted that compulsory withdrawal would have knocked out the eventual winner. Much would depend on the organizational strength of the parties dropping out. In France, the PCF can deliver almost the totality of its first round vote to a socialist candidate on the second round, but socialist votes on the first ballot are not so readily transferred in the opposite direction.

The systems considered so far in the appendix all view the constituency as having a single "will" or preference. Systems differ in their capacity to discover this preference and other methods of voting could be devised, but are not in actual use to date. (There is, for example, a system of "approval voting" [Brams and Fishburn, 1978.]). None of these claim to produce proportional results because they do not seek them. If one begins with the assumption that territorially defined constituencies are entirely arbitrary and enclose a wide variety of interests, then one would want to fraction the task of representing that constituency. This is what proportional systems claim to do and therefore require multi-member constituencies. In dual representation systems of the West German type, one level must be composed of multi-member constituencies.

Since this type has been extensively discussed in the text, this appendix will briefly examine only the single transferable vote system (used in the Republic of Ireland and in elections to the Australian senate) and the straight list type used in many smaller European countries.

Under STV, as under the AV system just examined, voters must rank-order their preferred candidates. As constituencies return three or more legislators, parties nominate more than one candidate in most cases and voters distribute their ranked preferences over candidates of their own and other parties. Unlike the AV case, votes are distributed from winners as well as losers, so a party's most popular candidate might pull other party candidates up with him. Counting proceeds as follows. (See also Jaensch, 1975).

First a quota is established, sufficient to elect a member to the parliament. This quota equals the threshold of exclusion: the number of votes cast, divided by one more than the number of seats to be filled from the constituency. Any candidate receiving more than the quota is declared elected and his surplus votes are redistributed according to the next available preference indicated. (One need not, at this point, go into the technical problems associated with this.) Then, the candidate with the fewest first preferences is dropped from the list and his total vote is reallocated among next available preferences. In a five-member constituency where 120,000 votes are cast, the quota is 20,000. Anyone with at least 20,000 first preferences is declared elected, and the reallocation of surplus votes and of the votes of lowest ranked candidates proceeds until five candidates have attained the quota (which may have been revised downward slightly to take account of the fact that not all voters provide full rank-orderings).

To see how proportionality is approximated, let us imagine a five-man constituency, where three parties each name five candidates. Suppose there are 12,000 voters, of whom 4,800 support party A, 4,800 support party B and 2,400 support party C. Let us suppose further that party A has an extremely popular candidate who draws 2,400 first preferences from his own party identifiers, 800 from identifiers with party B and 400 from identifiers of party C. With this exception let us suppose that all party identifiers reserve their first five preferences for members of their own party and that they scatter their preferences approximately randomly among their party's candidates.

The quota for election is thus 12,000 divided by 5 + 1 or 2,000 votes. With our assumptions, the count of first preferences should have Mr. A. Popular with 3,600, followed by the five candidates of party B clustered around 800 votes, followed by the other four candidates of party A at about 600 votes each and the five candidates of party C with about 400 votes each. Redistribution of Mr. A. Popular's surplus, will add about 1,075 votes to the aggregate for other A candidates, about 350 to the aggregate of the B candidates and approximately 175 to the aggregate of the C candidates. This will not bring any candidate up to the quota, and may not even change the remaining rank-ordering of candidate popularity very much. The five candidates of party C will still be at the bottom of the list, and will be eliminated one by one. Given our assumption about party-mindedness in the allocation of preferences, however, it must be the case that one candidate of party C will get over 2,000 votes since there are 2,400 identifiers. The remaining party A candidates will start to be eliminated, and, as they are, transferred votes will cause vote totals for the more successful A candidates to become intermingled with those of party B. Late eliminations will apply to candidates of both parties A and B, and eventually each will have attained two quotas. In this contrived example, perfect proportionality is achieved. With only five seats to be filled, it will usually be the case that exact proportionality is not achieved since it is doubtful that voters typically divide in the same ways that the number 5 can be divided into whole numbers.

In the last system, PR/LIST there may be only party and not candidate names. Even when candidates are named, a vote for a candidate is credited to his party and usually only exceptionally to him. Voters thus make a single mark, opposite the name of a party or candidate, on the ballot paper, regardless of the number of representatives to be elected from the district. Seats from the district are allocated in such a way as to reflect the proportion of the vote won by each party. If party A gets 40%, party B 33%, party C 16%, and party D 11%, and the district returns ten members, the top four candidates on the A list will be declared elected. So will the first three names on the B list, the first two names on the C list, and the first name on the D list.

This result is obtained by allocating the seats to minimize vote-to-seat ratios. The three principal ways of calculating these are the d'Hondt method, the St. Lagüe method, and the modified St. Lagüe method. The first, illustrated in appendix B, begins with the total vote won by each party in the district, which could be the whole country, a whole state or province, or some other area, and divides the vote by successive integers. The quotients thus obtained are rank-ordered and the district seats are given to the parties with the highest quotients. The St. Lagüe method obtains quotients by dividing only by successive odd integers. The modified St. Lagüe method obtains its first quotients by dividing the parties' votes by 1.4 rather than by 1. Though none of these methods change the results very much from strict proportionality, the St. Lagüe method does make it easier to win the first seat than to win subsequent seats. It is thus most favourable to small parties. The degree of favour is tempered in the modified version, while the d'Hondt system discriminates most sharply against small parties.

List proportional systems, in one version or other, are used in Holland, Belgium, Switzerland and the Scandinavian countries, among others. All allow the voter some opportunity to challenge the party's rank-ordering of candidates on the lists − the crucial determinant of election. In practice, it is very difficult for voters to assure the election of candidates they prefer but who are not highly placed. To do this, a very high degree of concerted action is necessary. (For a fuller description of these electoral systems and others, see Derek Urwin, 1978. Appraisals of some variants of proportional representation systems are made in Balinski and Young, 1978; and Lijphart and Gibberd, 1977).

Appendix B
Allocating 100 National Seats Among Provincial Party Lists

Imagine a dual representation system in which one hundred national seats are to be allocated proportionately to the national vote received by recognized political parties. In 1974, 99% of the total vote was received by such parties in the following proportions.

	% of Vote	% of National Seats
Liberal	43.6	44
Progressive Conservative	35.7	36
New Democratic Party	15.5	15
Social Credit	5.1	5

The question is now how the 44 Liberal seats, the 36 Progressive Conservative seats, etc. would be filled. Parties could be asked to name, for each province, a list of 30 or 40 people. The following example shows how the d'Hondt system could be used to allocate seats among the provincial lists. Beginning with the Liberals, the first line of quotients is calculated by dividing the total Liberal vote in each province by the number of seats won, plus one. Successive quotients are calculated by adding one to the current divisor. In this particular case, the 44 highest quotients win seats, filled from the appropriate provincial list. After having allocated the Liberal seats to Liberal lists, we go on to allocate seats among the lists put forth by other parties, up to the number of national seats won by each party.

As we see on the next page, the first three Liberal seats, denoted by superscripted letters, would have gone to the top names on the Alberta list, the fourth seat to the top name on the Nova Scotia list, the fifth seat back to Alberta, the sixth to Manitoba, and so on. For the Progressive Conservatives, the first seven seats go to Quebec, before Ontario qualifies for a seat, and it is not until the thirty-first quotient that any province other than these two get a seat.

Based on Liberal Vote, 1974

D*	NFLD.	P.E.I.	N.S.	N.B.	QUE.	ONT.	MAN.	SASK.	ALTA.	B.C.
n+1	16260	13466	52527[d]	19389	22172[oo]	29269[o]	40823[f]	31821[k]	168933[a]	37382[h]
n+2			39396[g]		21457	28242[p]	30618[m]	25456[aa]	84487[b]	33644[j]
n+3			31516[l]			27755[s]	24494[dd]	21214	56324[c]	30585[n]
n+4			26263[w]			27284[t]	20412		42243[e]	28036[r]
n+5			22512[ll]			26829[u]			33794[i]	25880[v]
n+6			19698			26390[v]			28162[q]	22429[mm]
n+7						25964[x]			24139[ff]	21027
n+8						25552[z]			21122	
n+9						25153[bb]				
n+10						24765[cc]				
n+11						24390[ee]				
n+12						24027[gg]				
n+13						23673[hh]				
n+14						23330[ii]				
n+15						22997[jj]				
n+16						22673[kk]				
n+17						22358[mm]				
n+18						22052[pp]				
n+19						21754[qq]				
n+20						21464[rr]				

* Signifies "divisor". n is the number of seats won by the party in the province. Superscripted letters indicate the order in which seats are allocated to provincial lists (aa follows z).

87

Based on Progressive Conservative Vote, 1974

D	NFLD.	P.E.I.	N.S.	N.B.	QUE.	ONT.	MAN.	SASK.	ALTA.	B.C.
n+1	18953	7144	20433	23733	130158[a]	48157[h]	21299	16761	20871	30282[ee]
n+2					104126[b]	46373[j]				28263[jj]
n+3					86722[c]	44717[k]				26497
n+4					74376[d]	43175[m]				
n+5					65079[e]	41736[n]				
n+6					57848[f]	40390[o]				
n+7					52063[g]	39128[q]				
n+8					47330[i]	37942[r]				
n+9					43386[l]	36826[t]				
n+10					40049[p]	35774[u]				
n+11					37189[s]	34780[v]				
n+12					34709[w]	33840[x]				
n+13					32540[z]	32950[y]				
n+14					30625[cc]	32105[aa]				
n+15					28924[hh]	31302[bb]				
n+16					27402	30539[dd]				
n+17						29811[ff]				
n+18						29118[gg]				
n+19						28456[ii]				
n+20						27824				

Based on NDP Votes, 1974

D	NFLD.	P.E.I.	N.S.	N.B.	QUE.	ONT.	MAN.	SASK.	ALTA.	B.C.
n+1	16445	2660	21735	24869	162080[a]	75568[d]	34943	43463[o]	63310[f]	77516[c]
n+2					81040[b]	68011[e]		32598	31655	58137[h]
n+3					54027[j]	61828[g]				46509[m]
n+4					40520	56676[i]				38758
n+5						52316[k]				
n+6						48580[l]				
n+7						45341[n]				
n+8						42507				

Based on Social Credit Votes, 1974

D	NFLD.	P.E.I.	N.S.	N.B.	QUE.	ONT.	MAN.	SASK.	ALTA.	B.C.
n+1	143		1457	8407	35002[a]	6575	4750	4539	22909	12433
n+2					32309[b]					
n+3					30001[c]					
n+4					28001[d]					
n+5					26251[e]					

89

Appendix C
Analysis of the 1979 Federal Election

The plurality electoral system exaggerates the number of seats won by the leading vote-getter in any area. It tends to penalize second and third place parties especially where these attempt a national appeal. These propositions were demonstrated for the 1968-74 periods in table 1 in the main text. They were true again in 1979 as we see in table C-1. The

Table C-1

The Ratio of Percentage of Seats to Percentage of Votes, Canada and Provinces, 1979

	LIB.	P.C.	NDP	S.C.	OTHER
Canada	*1.01**	1.34	0.52	0.47	0/1.5**
Newfoundland	*1.51*	0.93	0.45		
Prince Edward Is.	0/40.3	*1.90*	0/7.0		0/0.1
Nova Scotia	0.77	*1.40*	0.48		0/0.4
New Brunswick	*1.34*	1.00	0/15.3		0/0.1
Quebec	*1.44*	0.20	0/5.1	0.50	0/3.8
Ontario	0.92	*1.44*	0.30		0/0.7
Manitoba	0.61	*1.15*	1.10	0/0.2	0/0.3
Saskatchewan	0/19.9	*1.69*	0.78	0/0.5	0/0.8
Alberta	0/20.7	*1.50*	0/10.3	0/1.0	0/1.5
British Col.	0.16	*1.52*	0.90	0/0.2	0/0.6
Yukon-NWT	0/32.6	*1.80*	1.21		0/1.0

Source: Ratioes are calculated from vote and seat figures communicated by Canadian Press on May 24, 1979. Recounts and the official count could lead to slightly different figures.

* The popular vote leader in each jurisdiction is shown in italics.

** An entry of the form 0/x.y indicates that no seats were won for x.y percent of the vote.

Liberals led in popular vote in Newfoundland, New Brunswick and Quebec. In those provinces, and only in those provinces, did they obtain a bonus of parliamentary seats (indicated by a ratio greater than 1 in the table). In all other provinces, they received fewer seats than their vote would have produced under a proportional system. In Prince Edward Island, Saskatchewan, Alberta, and the North, they obtained no seats at all, though gaining upward of 20 percent of the popular vote.

The New Democratic Party was dealt an equally harsh blow in the six eastern provinces: shut out in Quebec, New Brunswick and Prince Edward Island, obtaining only half its proportional seat entitlement in Nova Scotia and Newfoundland, and one-third its proper number of seats in Ontario. It was also shut out in Alberta, but got very close to its proportional number of seats in the other western provinces.

The major beneficiary of the electoral system in 1979 was the Progressive Conservative party. It obtained a larger proportion of seats than votes in Prince Edward Island, Nova Scotia, and all provinces from Ontario westward. Such bonuses are guaranteed to the leading party in seven provinces (and the North). Comparing table C-1 with table 1, we see that the 1979 ratioes are about the same size as those usually observed for leading parties. The electoral system does exaggerate regional polarization. It continued to do so in 1979, but not to an unusual degree. That we have observed a much sharper polarization than in the past is due to real vote movements, as well as to the electoral system. The ratioes of 1.44 for Ontario and 1.60 for British Columbia are the largest since 1968, however, and certainly contributed to the Clark victory.

The electoral system continues to penalize the Progressive Conservative party in Quebec, though again, not to an atypical degree. The party obtained only one-fifth as many seats as it would have under strict proportionality. There would have been no problem finding cabinet material from that province had the electoral system proposed in this study been in place.

To see how the proposed system might have worked in 1979, we have simulated the results of that election under the new electoral system. As with the simulation underlying table 7 in the text, we have had to turn to some dubious assumptions to simplify our task. Expecting the parties to have had the same rate of success in winning constituencies as they did under the present electoral system does not unduly strain one's credulity, though we can't know exactly how the new constituency boundaries would be drawn. Expecting the vote distribution to remain the same under the new electoral system is a much more questionable proposition, but alternative assumptions are too numerous to consider. The results of the simulation, reported in table C-2, should be taken as indicative rather than definitive.

Table C-2

*A Simulation of the 1979 Federal Election
under the System Proposed in the Test*

Prov.	MP TYPE	LIB.	P.C.	NDP	S.C.	OTHER	TOTAL
NFLD.	const.	3	1	1			5
	prov.		2	2			4
	total	3	3	3			9
P.E.I.	const.		3				3
	prov.	2					2
	total	2	3				5
N.B.	const.	4	3				7
	prov.	1	2	2			5
	total	5	5	2			12
N.S.	const.	2	4	1			7
	prov.	3	2	2			7
	total	5	6	3			14
QUE.	const.	45	1		4		50
	prov.	13	12	5	11	3	44
	total	58	13	5	15	3	94
ONT.	const.	21	38	4			63
	prov.	23	12	21			56
	total	44	50	25			119
MAN.	const.	1	5	3			9
	prov.	3	3	3			9
	total	4	8	6			18
SASK.	const.		7	2			9
	prov.	3	1	5			9
	total	3	8	7			18
ALTA.	const.		14				14
	prov.	6	3	3			12
	total	6	17	3			26
B.C.	const.		14	5			19
	prov.	8	2	6			16
	total	8	16	11			35
NORTH	const.		1	1			2
	prov.	1	1				2
	total	1	2	1			4
CANADA	seats (%)	39.2	37.0	18.6	4.2	0.8	
	vote (%)	39.9	36.1	17.9	4.5	1.5	
	seats (%)(actual)	40.4	48.2	9.2	2.1	0.0	

They are, nonetheless, quite interesting. The Progressive Conservatives would have been entitled to thirteen seats in Quebec, ten percent of its total caucus. Under the present system, less than two percent of its caucus is from Quebec. The Liberals would have been entitled to thirteen seats on the Prairies and a further eight in British Columbia. Fifteen percent of its caucus might have come from the west, whereas only two percent does. Either party, then, could have constructed a representative cabinet. Since their additional seats in these weak regions would have been filled by list nominees, one presumes that the parties would have elected their strongest candidates.

To form a government, both parties would have had to reach some agreement with the NDP. This would have been the only swing party in the 31st parliament. It comes close to occupying that position today since a Progressive Conservative plus Créditiste combination has only a tenuous hold on a parliamentary majority. In the short run, the NDP gets the major benefit in terms of additional seats. In view of the reaction of various business groups to the 1979 outcome, this is clearly an obstacle to achieving electoral system reform.

From the last three lines of table C-2, some bias in attributing seats still remains in the proposed system. It is much smaller than under the present electoral system, and it is in a desirable direction. The proposed electoral system slightly rewards parties who maintain strength in the most provinces. The Progressive Conservatives and the NDP gain a slightly larger proportion of seats than votes; other parties, a slightly smaller one.

Finally, comparing table C-2 with our previous simulation of the 1974 results allows us to gauge the dynamic quality of the proposed electoral system. The changing preferences of the electorate are quite accurately reflected. The Liberals would have lost 21 seats outside Quebec, partly offsetting these by a gain of 7 in that province. The Progressive Conservative party would have gained 12 seats, 8 of them in Ontario, but would have lost 10 seats, 7 of these in Quebec. The first result clearly reflects the Liberal campaign − the stress on national unity and the subordination of economic or social themes. The second result is also a faithful reflection of the priorities of the Progressive Conservative campaign.

This, of course, emphasizes the limits of the simulation. Both campaigns could well have been different had the new electoral system been operative. Given the actual campaigns, the new electoral system would have denied the Progressive Conservatives their victory. On the other hand, we should note that the Progressive Conservative campaign did not cost them much in Quebec − only one seat, under the present electoral rules. They therefore had no real incentive to maintain their Quebec vote at even its 1974 level. Under the proposed new electoral system, the Progressive Conservatives would have had only to maintain their 1974 vote in Quebec to have been the largest parliamentary party. Under the new electoral system, as under the old, the Progressive Conservatives could have earned the right to form a government.

Bibliography

Acton, J.E.E.D. (1956) Essays on Freedom and Power. G. Himmelfarb (ed.) New York: Meridian Books.

Aitkin, Don and Michael Kahan (1974) "Australia: Class Politics in the New World," pp. 437-480 in R. Rose (ed.) Electoral Behavior: A Comparative Handbook. New York: The Free Press.

Bain, H.M. and D.S. Hecock (1957) Ballot Position and Voter's Choice. Detroit: Wayne State University Press.

Balinski, M.K. and H.P. Young (1978) "Stability, Coalitions and Schisms in Proportional Representation Systems." American Political Science Review 72:848-858.

Barry, Brian (1970) Sociologists, Economists and Democracy. London: Collier-Macmillan.

Berrington, H. (1975) "Electoral Reform and National Government," pp. 269-292 in S. Finer (1975).

Blondel, Jean (1968) "Party Systems and Patterns of Government in Western Democracies." Canadian Journal of Political Science 1:180-203.

Brams, Steven J. and Peter C. Fishburn "Approval Voting." American Political Science Review 72:831-847.

Browne, Eric (1971) "Testing Theories of Coalition Formation in the European Context." Comparative Political Studies 3:391-411.

Cairns, Alan C. (1968) "The Electoral System and the Party System in Canada, 1921-1965." Canadian Journal of Political Science 1:55-80.

——— (1970) "A Reply to J.A.A. Lovink." Canadian Journal of Political Science 3:517-521.

Carty, R.K. (1976) Partisan Allegiance and Parochial Association. Unpublished Ph.D. thesis, Queen's University.

——— (forthcoming) "Electoral Laws and Electoral Competition in Ireland."

Clarke, Harold D. et al (1979) Political Choice in Canada. Scarborough, Ont.: McGraw-Hill Ryerson.

Converse, Phillip (1962) "Information Flow and the Stability of Party Attitudes." Public Opinion Quarterly 26:578-599.

Courtney, John C. (1978) "Recognition of Canadian Political Parties in Parliament and in Law." Canadian Journal of Political Science 11:33-60.

Cowart, A. (1978a) "The Economic Policies of European Governments, Part I: Monetary Policy." British Journal of Political Science 8:285-311.

——— (1978b) "The Economic Policies of European Governments, Part II: Fiscal Policy." British Journal of Political Science 8:425-439.

Crewe, Ivor (1975) "Electoral Reform and the Local M.P." pp. 317-342 in S. Finer (1975).

Daalder, Hans (forthcoming) "The Netherlands," in Stanley Henig and John Pinder (eds.) European Political Parties. (2nd edition) London: Allen and Unwin.

Denver, D.T. and H.T.G. Hands (1974) "Marginality and Turnout in British General Elections." British Journal of Political Science 4:17-35.

Dewachter, Wilfrid (1978) "Recent Changes in the Belgian Party System." (mimeo).

Downs, Anthony (1957) An Economic Theory of Democracy. Chicago: Harper and Row.

Duverger, Maurice (1951) Political Parties. (trans. B. and R. North) New York: Wiley Science Editions.

Elkins, David (1978) "Party Identification: a Conceptual Analysis." Canadian Journal of Political Science 11:419-435.

Evenson, Jeff and Richard Simeon (1978) "The Roots of Discontent." Paper presented to the Workshop on the Political Economy of Confederation, forthcoming by the Economic Council of Canada.

Finer, Samuel (1975) Adversary Politics and Electoral Reform. London: Anthony Wigram.

Hermens, F.A. (1941) Democracy or Anarchy? Notre Dame, Ind.: University of Notre Dame Press.

Irvine, W.P. (1975) "Explaining the Brittleness of Partisanship in Canada." Unpublished paper presented at the Annual Meeting, Canadian Political Science Association.

——— (1976) "Testing Explanations of Voting Turnout in Canada," pp. 335-351 in Ian Budge et al Party Identification and Beyond. London: John Wiley and Sons.

——— (1977) "Liberté, Egalité, Efficacité: Respecifying the Federal Role," pp. 169-176 in Richard Simeon (ed.) Must Canada Fail? Montreal: McGill-Queen's University Press.

Irvine, W.P. and H. Gold (1979) "Do Frozen Cleavages Ever Go Stale?" British Journal of Political Science.

Jaensch, D. (1975) "Australian Electoral Systems," pp. 366-378 in Richard Lucy (ed.) The Pieces of Politics. Melbourne: MacMillan.

Johnston, Richard and Janet Ballantyne (1977) "Geography and the Electoral System." Canadian Journal of Political Science 10:857-866.

Kamin, Leon (1958) "Ethnic and Party Affiliations of Candidates as Determinants of Voting." Canadian Journal of Psychology 12. Reprinted pp. 191-198 in John C. Courtney (ed.) Voting in Canada. Scarborough: Prentice Hall.

Kim, J.O., S. Enokson and J. Petrocik (1975) "Voter Turnout among the American States." American Political Science Review 69:107-123.

Leduc, Lawrence (1977) "Political Behaviour and the Issue of Majority Government in Two Federal Elections." Canadian Journal of Political Science 10:311-339.

Leduc, L. et al (1976) "Partisanship, Political Interest and Electoral Campaigns in Canada." Unpublished paper delivered at the Edinburgh IPSA Congress.

Laponce, Jean (1957) "The Protection of Minorities by the Electoral System." Western Political Quarterly 10:318-339.

Lehmbruch, G. (1977) "Liberal Corporatism and Party Government." Comparative Political Studies 10:91-126.

Lijphart, A. and Roger Gibberd (1977) "Thresholds and Payoffs in List Systems of Proportional Representation." European Journal of Political Research 5:219-244.

Lipset, S.M. (1976) "Radicalism in North America," Transactions of the Royal Society of Canada IV, 14:19-55.

Lovink, J.A.A. (1970) "On Analysing the Impact of the Electoral System on the Party System." Canadian Journal of Political Science 3:497-516.

——— (1973) "Is Canadian Politics Too Competitive?" Canadian Journal of Political Science 6:341-79.

Meisel, J. (1963) "The Stalled Omnibus." Social Forces 30:367-90.

——— (1978) "The Decline of Party in Canada," pp. 119-135 in H.G. Thorburn (ed.) Party Politics in Canada. (4th ed.) Scarborough: Prentice-Hall of Canada.

Neilson, W.A.W. and J.C. MacPherson (1978) The Legislative Process in Canada: The Need for Reform. Montreal: Institute for Research on Public Policy.

O'Leary, C. (1975) "Ireland: The North and the South," pp. 153-183 in S. Finer (1975).

Perlin, G. (forthcoming) A Party Divided. Montreal: McGill-Queen's University Press.

Qualter, T. (1968) "Seats and Votes: an Application of the Cube Law to the Canadian Electoral System." Canadian Journal of Political Science 1:336-344.

Rabushka, A. and K. Shepsle (1972) Politics in Plural Societies. Columbus, Ohio: Charles Merrill.

Rae, D.W. (1967) The Political Consequences of Electoral Laws. New Haven: Yale University Press.

Rae, D.W., V. Hanby and J. Loosemore (1971) "Thresholds of Representation and Thresholds of Exclusion." Comparative Political Studies 3:479-488.

Riker, W.H. (1962) The Theory of Political Coalitions. New Haven: Yale University Press.

Roberts, G.K. (1975) "The Federal Republic of Germany," pp. 203-222 in S. Finer (1975).

Robertson, David (1976) A Theory of Party Competition. London: John Wiley and Sons.

Robson, C. and B. Walsh (1974) "The Importance of Positional Voting Bias in the Irish General Election of 1973." Political Studies 22:191-203.

Rose, Richard (1976) The Problem of Party Government. Harmondsworth: Penguin ed.

Rose, Richard and D. Urwin (1970) "Persistence and Change in Party Systems." Political Studies 18:287-319.

Sankoff, D. and K. Mellos (1973) "La Régionalisation Electorale et l'Amplification des Proportions." Canadian Journal of Political Science 6:380-398.

Sartori, G. (1966) "European Political Parties: the Case of Polarized Pluralism," pp. 137-76 in J. Lapalombara and M. Weiner (eds.) Political Parties and Political Development. Princeton, N.J.: Princeton University Press.

——— (1976) Parties and Party Systems. Cambridge, Eng.: Cambridge University Press.

Simeon, Richard (1978) "Criteria for Choice." Paper presented to the Workshop on the Political Economy of Confederation, forthcoming by the Economic Council of Canada.

Smiley, Donald V. (1978) "Federalism and the Legislative Process in Canada," pp. 73-87 in Neilson and MacPherson (1978).

Smith, David (1977) "Intra-Party Reform and Regional Decline: the Liberals on the Prairies." Unpublished paper presented at the Annual Meeting of the Canadian Political Science Association.

Spafford, Duff (1970) "The Electoral System of Canada." American Political Science Review 64:168-176.

——— (1972) "Two Notes on the Theory of Multi-Party Systems." Unpublished paper presented to the Annual Meeting of the Canadian Political Science Association.

——— (1974) " 'Wasted' Votes in Three-Party Contests." Unpublished paper presented to the Annual Meeting of the Canadian Political Science Association.

Stout, D.K. (1975) "Incomes Policy and the Costs of the Adversary System," pp. 117-140 in S. Finer (1975).

Taebel, Delbert A. (1975) "The Effect of Ballot Position on Electoral Success." American Journal of Political Science 19:519-526.

Taylor, M. and V. Herman (1971) "Party Systems and Government Stability." American Political Science Review 65:28-37.

Tufte, E. (1973) "The Relationship between Seats and Votes in Two-Party Systems." American Political Science Review 67:540-554.

——— (1978) Political Control of the Economy. Princeton, N.J.: Princeton University Press.

Upton, G.J.G. and D. Brook (1974) "The Importance of Positional Voting in British Elections." Political Studies 22:178-190.

Walker, Jack L. (1966) "Ballot Forms and Voter Fatigue: An Analysis of the Office Block and Party Column Ballots." Midwest Journal of Political Science 10:448-464.

Whitaker, Reginald (1977) The Government Party. Toronto: University of Toronto Press.

Wilson, T. (1975) "The Economic Costs of the Adversary System," pp. 99-116 in S. Finer (1975).